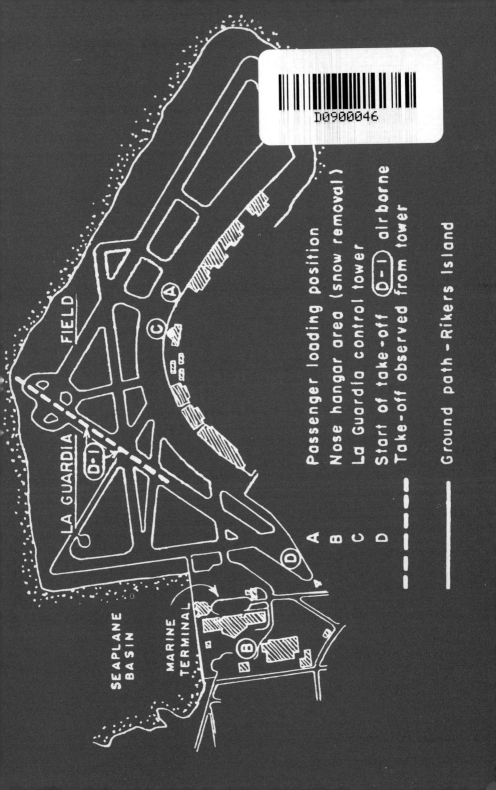

LA GUARDIA FIELD

SEAPLANE BASIN

MARINE TERMINAL

A Passenger loading position
B Nose hangar area (snow removal)
C La Guardia control tower
D Start of take-off D-1 airborne
    Take-off observed from tower

- - - - - Ground path – Rikers Island

Tiger On A Leash

By the author of COLLISION COURSE

Tiger On A Leash

ALVIN MOSCOW

G. P. Putnam's Sons   New York

for

H. C.

Illustrations will be found following page 128.

Tiger On A Leash

THE airline industry, a toddling infant before World War II, was booming with the vitality of adolescence in 1957. The jet age was around the corner. Air travel already had become a way of life in the United States. Each day more than 134,500 persons went from one place to another by commercial plane, so that by the end of the year, the statisticians would count up more than 49 million passengers flown almost one billion miles by fifty-five airlines. The airplane had become as available as the railroad or motorbus and on almost every airliner every day you could find among its passengers a cross-section of American life.

However, while air travel had increased forty-fold in the preceding eighteen years, the fear of flying persisted in most people.

Mrs. Mary Bourgoin, an alert, cheerful housewife in Augusta, Maine, had not slept well the night before she and her husband were to fly to Florida on Friday, February 1. She had flown often but she had premonitions about this trip and they manifested themselves in minor ways. She left her suitcases unpacked until the last minute. She delayed washing her hair in case the trip should be called off. She de-

Chapter One

cided to leave the dry cleaner's tags on her clothes so that, if necessary, they could be used for identification. When she left her nine-month-old daughter Kathy with the child's grandmother, she consciously said "good-by" when she might just as easily have said, "See you Sunday."

The Bourgoins, Mary and Arthur, were going to Miami Beach for a long weekend. Of modest means, they could afford the trip because it was virtually free. Arthur Bourgoin was a ticket agent for Northeast Airlines in Augusta and he and his wife could travel on a pass, paying only a service charge of about $2. Almost everyone employed by the airline was taking or trying to take advantage of Northeast Airlines' new bonanza. The company had just won the most coveted air route in the United States—New York City to Miami and other Florida points. This was the Golden Route: it had earned fortunes for Eastern Airlines and National Airlines. As Florida real estate and tourism had boomed since the end of World War II, so had air travel between New York and Miami. Close to one million passengers flew each year between those two cities, making the route the most heavily traveled between any two major cities in the United States.

There was still another fortune to be made on the Golden Route, it seemed, and since the end of the war, eleven airlines had petitioned the Civil Aeronautics Board for a certificate of necessity that would add a third airline to the New York–Miami service. The battle for the route had gone on for five years, and Northeast won. The new route gave the small New England airline a dazzling opportunity to enter the big league of air transportation. The prize doubled Northeast's potential earnings. It also doubled its problems.

The new route directly concerned most of the airline's

employees in the promises it implied of higher individual earnings and better working conditions. It also charged the atmosphere throughout the company with the thrill of a challenge, the thrill of becoming Big Time. More immediately, it offered employees virtually free travel up and down the coast from Maine to Florida.

Arthur Bourgoin and his wife, flying down to Boston on an old twin-engine DC-3 to connect with a 10 A.M. flight to New York and Miami, were not the only Northeast Airlines people heading for Florida that first day of February. At Boston's Logan International Airport, the Bourgoins met several friends among the Northeast families aboard the company's luxurious new DC-6B.

Mary Bourgoin renewed an old friendship with Dorothy Richardson, the airline's chief stewardess, a slender, vivacious blonde who looked ten years younger than her thirty-five years. Beside the chief stewardess sat her husband, Bill, a flight engineer for Northeast, and their young son, Wayne. Behind them sat her father, mother and younger sister.

Dorothy Richardson, who had resigned as a stewardess after seven years with Northeast to marry in 1952, had returned to the company the following year as chief stewardess. In her new post, she had to train, supervise, sometimes discipline and almost always "mother" her charges. An airline is far more like a family than are most businesses, and Northeast, as a small outfit, was even more familylike than its large competitors. Mrs. Richardson had plenty of "mothering" to do.

Now she was on her way to Florida to conduct a week-long training course for stewardesses who had to meet government standards to qualify for the company's new DC-6s. For her mother, father and sister, the trip was a vacation. It was their first trip to Florida and the chief stewardess, an observant young woman, had noted her father's nervousness at the Boston airport. Norman Chadwick, a jovial man with a zest for life that disguised his sixty-two years, had been unusually quiet and withdrawn when the family gathered at the airport. It seemed almost as though he did not want to make the trip. But his wife, Laura, and his younger daughter, Gloria, were delighted at the idea of a midwinter week in the sun.

Farther back in the plane sat a young, eager Northeast stewardess for whom Dorothy Richardson felt a special responsibility. She was Emily Gately, a tall, slender girl twenty-one years old with bright blue eyes, blond hair and a ready smile. But her smile cloaked a determination without which she might never have realized her ambition to fly.

Soon after her graduation from high school in Boston, Emily Gately had sought a job as a stewardess. But she weighed only 108 pounds, too little for a girl who stood five-feet-seven. Airline after airline turned her away. So she enrolled in a private training school for stewardesses and ground personnel. Devotedly, she devoured mountains of food and oceans of milkshakes, cream and evaporated milk which she detested. But she made the weight at 112 pounds and with the help of Dottie Richardson, who taught at the school in her spare time, landed a job as probationary stewardess with Northeast Airlines. In qualifying for the job, she found it barely possible to lift and remove a forty-pound emergency exit door in the time allowed and she almost flunked out. Next, she became seasick while going through her overwater ditching test, and then, when she made her first flight as a stewardess, she became airsick. It had been a memorable trip from Boston to New York, for she had been the only one aboard the plane who had been ill.

For the next five months, every time she went up Emily Gately had been sick. As a beginner, she had the least desirable schedule of short flights and she usually made half a dozen landings and take-offs a day. Throughout the airline, they called her the Airsick Kid. She lived on saltine crackers and nausea pills and the trip to the lavatory with the paper bag became routine.

Then, suddenly, flying became a delightful experience. Her airsickness disappeared and her love for flying became unbounded. Two months later, on January 31, Chief Stewardess Richardson informed her she was to start a six-month tour of duty out of Florida the next day, flying with one of the airline's senior stewardesses, Doris Steele, so that she could be trained while she worked. Emily complained that she needed time to pack her clothes in Boston and she was given a 24-hour delay. So Emily Gately, seven months a stewardess, was flying deadhead to New York to connect there with Northeast's afternoon Flight 823 to Miami. Meanwhile, in Miami, Doris Steele, a short, dynamic blonde of thirty-four, had enlisted another stewardess, Kay Virchow, with whom she had flown during January, for the one round trip. Miss Virchow, a good-looking brunette who was planning to leave the airline soon to be married, agreed to make the extra flight as a favor.

There were several other Northeast employees on the 10 A.M. flight out of Boston, heading for Miami and hoping not to be bumped by paying customers during the stopover at New York's La Guardia Airport. Gerald Lassell, a slender twenty-five-year-old instrument mechanic, had his blond wife, Marilyn, and their eighteen-month-old son, Roy, along for a weekend in Miami. He wanted to take a look at

Florida to decide whether he would ask for a transfer to the airline's maintenance base being set up there.

John Reddington, a Northeast ticket agent in Boston, also was going down for a quick look at Miami with his wife. Blanche Zukowski, wife of the Northeast station manager at the Worcester (Massachusetts) Airport, intended to catch up on some fun in Miami with two girl friends. Her husband had flown there two weeks before for a hasty company conference on exploiting the new route during the current winter season and he had not been able to take his wife. Mrs. Zukowski had flown before and admitted no fear of flying, but she had long made it a practice to pray on every take-off and landing.

Mrs. Esther Chopelas, a Malden, Massachusetts, housewife, was full of trepidation that day. She was going up in an airplane for the first time in her life. A former waitress, she had married the owner of the restaurant who had nine children from his first marriage and she had brought into this world eight children of her own. The trip to Florida with her youngest son, Gregory, who was two and one-half, was a gift from her husband, Stavros. He had driven to Miami two weeks before.

Like most people who travel infrequently, Mrs. Chopelas had made her vacation arrangements through a local travel agent who had booked her on Northeast Flight 823, leaving La Guardia Airport in New York at 2:45 P.M., February 1, nonstop to Miami. The connecting flight from Boston to New York was via American Airlines. Her husband's brother, George, drove her from Malden to Logan Airport in Boston, and as the time drew near for departure she was shaking with apprehension.

"If you're so nervous, why don't you take out some insurance?" asked her brother-in-law, pointing to a vending machine.

"Not on your life," Mrs. Chopelas replied. "It's almost like asking for trouble."

On the hour-long flight to New York, Mrs. Chopelas was so nervous that the stewardess sat by her side, comforting her.

In Norwich, Connecticut, that morning, John Q. Nolan, a stocky twenty-five-year-old sophomore at the University of Miami, who also had booked passage on Flight 823 through a local travel agent, chose to go to New York by train. Nolan, who was majoring in aviation administration at the University's School of Business, had flown home a week before to attend the funerals of his father and of his favorite aunt, who had died within a day of one another. But life goes on for the living, and John Q. Nolan was eager to return to Florida. He and his college roommate had a double-date for that evening and his friends would be waiting for him at Miami Airport.

The situation was reversed for another passenger booked for Flight 823. Miss Lillian Nixon, a thin woman of fifty-six who wore rimless spectacles, was going to Florida for the funeral of her foster mother, who had died two days before in a nursing home in St. Petersburg. Miss Nixon, who lived quietly and alone in a little flat, was nevertheless well known to hundreds of people in Worcester because she had been telephone operator at the Worcester *Post and Gazette* for the past twenty-two years.

For the New Englanders who started out early in the morning to make connections with Flight 823 the day had begun with beautiful weather, though the sun was obscured occasionally by what weather forecasters like to call variable cloudiness. John Nolan, for instance, wore no over-coat so that he would be dressed for Miami climate on his date that evening.

But by noon, light snow began to fall and a winter fog rolled in over the New York metropolitan area. The snow did not worry Mason Benson, a handsome, six-foot-four, former college basketball star, and his beautiful wife as they left their Park Avenue apartment for Flight 823. Their only concern was the possibility that the flight might be canceled because of the weather, cutting further into their ten-day vacation. They were looking forward to joining Mrs. Benson's family in Miami. The Bensons had canceled their first-class tickets on another airline two days before because of the unexpected arrival in the city of an important out-of-town business customer. Then they had booked on the first available daytime flight after January 30, which was Northeast Flight 823. The Bensons were both experienced air travelers. As salesman in charge of the western and southwestern territory of a large doll company, Benson had flown thousands of hours and his wife, Peggy, who frequently joined him on holidays, had logged hundreds of hours in the air.

A change of business plans also brought Edwin J. Dresner, a wealthy Long Island building contractor, to Flight 823. Dresner, who took a Florida vacation every winter, had canceled his reservations on a first-class flight the week before because of business. He booked two seats for his wife and himself on Northeast only because they seemed to be the only seats available for February 1, the first day he could get away. A determined businessman accustomed to having his own way, he called the airline directly for reservations. He asked the type of equipment used for the flight and he was told it was a DC-6A. He booked reservations, thinking that a DC-6A was merely a later model of the four-engined DC-6.

Sheer chance brought Kenneth Kronen, a twenty-nine-year-old textile salesman and his young family to Flight 823. The Kronens, who lived in a small home about a half hour's drive from La Guardia Airport, were being driven there by Mrs. Kronen's brother to catch a 9 A.M. National Airlines flight for Miami. The talk in the car was animated and the driver missed a turn. By the time they got to the airport, National Airlines had relinquished the Kronens' reservations to stand-bys. The National plane was still at the ramp, but reservations usually are held only until a half hour before departure time.

The distraught Kronens, carrying their two boys, Ricky, two and a half, and Mark, six weeks old, checked every scheduled flight to Miami. They were anxious to reach Selma Kronen's parents before sundown that Friday, wanting not to travel after the Jewish Sabbath began. National Airlines had seats available only on a night flight. Eastern Airlines was booked solid through the day and night. The Kronens were recommended to Northeast Airlines, of which they had never heard, and were offered a choice of reserved seats for the afternoon flight, scheduled to arrive in Miami at 6:45 P.M. It would still be light there. Kenneth Kronen inspected a seating plan and chose two seats over the left wing. He considered that the best and safest location in the plane, and he was quite pleased at his luck.

At New York International Airport, better known as Idlewild Airport, a nonscheduled carrier, Trans-American Airlines, canceled a flight to Miami because of mechanical trouble and five passengers chose to transfer to Northeast's 823, leaving from La Guardia, rather than go to Newark Airport in New Jersey for another TAA flight.

And so, for a variety of reasons, a small cross-section of American people headed for Northeast Airlines Flight 823 on February 1, 1957. Some passengers were scared at the prospect of flying. Some felt no conscious fear. Yet every air traveler, consciously or not, feels a tingle of apprehension at the thought of being enclosed in a 100,000-pound metal cylinder hurtling through the air four miles above the earth. The fear is rooted in a feeling of helplessness: if anything happens, a passenger can do nothing to save himself. The fear is based not on reason but on emotion.

Reason would assure anyone that the airliner, with all its safeguards, is just as safe as the motorbus or the railroad and much safer than the family automobile. The chance of being killed in a commercial airliner is almost infinitesimal. The passenger fatality rate on scheduled airlines each year has been less than one person per hundred million passenger miles flown. In this year, 1957, for instance, thirty passengers would lose their lives on domestic flights, seventy in motorbus accidents, seventeen in railroad accidents, and 25,700 in automobiles. The accident fatality *rate* per billion passenger miles of travel in 1957 came to twelve in domestic scheduled airline planes, thirteen in buses, seven in trains and 260 in cars and taxicabs.

Airline flying has become so safe that commercial airline pilots pay no extra premium for life insurance. Their occupation is not considered hazardous. In fact, one insurance company has calculated that if a purely statistical pilot were to fly until the law of averages trapped him in a fatal accident, he would have to fly until he was a thousand years old.

The statistics reflect the result of the efforts of the entire aviation industry toward safety. Most passengers, however, are ignorant of the thousands of government regulations, the rigid procedures and safety practices of the airlines, the high standards of design ruling the manufacture of every component part of an airplane. Of all modes of transportation the airline industry is the most safety-conscious.

But when a passenger buys a ticket for any one flight of any one airline, he performs an act of faith. He is neither qualified nor does he have the opportunity to judge the plane, the crew or the airline management. He cannot look over the shoulder of the mechanic servicing the airplane. He cannot look up the pilot's flying record. When he buys his ticket, a passenger puts his faith in the reputation of the airline and indirectly in the government agencies which regulate the airlines for the safety of the public.

Thus, ninety-five passengers, including eleven children, would board Northeast Airlines Flight 823 for a scheduled four-hour flight to Miami. Few if any of them would or could have any idea that the airliner was a converted cargo plane which had been grounded the day before because of propeller trouble; that the captain was probably the only airline pilot who had crashed twice before and was still flying; that the co-pilot was making his first trip in a DC-6; that the flight engineer was a ground mechanic two weeks out of flight school; or that Northeast Airlines had started the New York–Florida route using four-engine equipment for the first time less than three weeks before.

Chapter Two

NORTHEAST had built its reputation slowly over twenty-four years as the "Yankee Fleet" and "New England's Own Airline." In its competition with other airlines that served the major cities of the Northeast—among them American Airlines, the largest domestic carrier—it appealed to the local loyalties of New Englanders.

Northeast was a small, friendly operation somewhat reminiscent of the old barnstorming days of aviation. Its pilots and senior employees were individuals; they had not been swallowed up by a big corporation. Almost everyone knew everyone else on a first-name basis. Pilots of other airlines knew they could usually hitch a ride on a Northeast plane because there were always available space and a friendly pilot. Yet, the Northeast operation was a safe one. The Yankee Fleet held a perfect record for passenger safety dating back to 1933 when it was established as the Boston–Maine Airways, serving points between Boston, Maine and Montreal. Amelia Earhart, a New Englander and the most famous woman pilot in the United States, had been one of its founders.

Jacqueline Cochrane, perhaps the second best-known aviatrix, was a director. Her husband, Floyd B. Odlum, controlled the airline financially as chairman and chief executive officer of Atlas Corporation, one of the nation's largest holding companies, which was majority stockholder in Northeast. Howard Hughes, the famous aviator who controls Trans-World Airlines through the Hughes Tool Company, also was an important stockholder of Atlas Corp.

Of the nation's twelve trunk airlines holding permanent operating rights over high-density traffic routes, Northeast was the smallest and the poorest. It had been losing money for years simply because it had the poorest pick of air routes. Although its operations were extended to New York City in 1944, most of the thirty-six cities it served were in New England. Almost all of them were beset by storms, fog and the worst conceivable flying weather. Business fell off so drastically every winter that Northeast was virtually a seasonal airline. Among its one thousand employees, it had only about 125 pilots and co-pilots, some 40 or 50 of whom were part-time fliers, furloughed back to ground jobs during the winter.

In an industry dominated by four-engine aircraft in 1957, Northeast operated only a small fleet of twin-engine planes. It had twelve DC-3s, each with a capacity of only twenty-one passengers, and five Convair 240s, each of which could carry only forty paying customers.

As a trunk line carrying mail, it was required to serve the small cities of Vermont, New Hampshire and Maine. All three states together did not offer the potential business of one city the size of Detroit. It had to provide for itself many of the services, such as weather forecasting, that the government furnished at large, big-city airports. In Lebanon, New Hampshire, for example, the Northeast ticket agent acted also as weather observer. Before a flight for Lebanon departed from Boston, the ticket agent was obliged to dash outside, estimate the ceiling, visibility and general weather, then dash back to his office to teletype the information to Boston. But the root of Northeast's financial problems was that its flights throughout New England were short hauls, and the moneymaking flights are the long ones. Worse, the short flight encountered severe competition from railroads, buses and private cars. As a result, when most airlines were at their financial healthiest, Northeast needed and received a government subsidy of approximately $2,000,000 a year to keep it solvent.

It was this subsidy which, probably more than any other single factor, won the Golden Route for Northeast. Northeast's ten rival applicants for the route had included Pan American Airways—economically and politically the most powerful airline in the world—but the CAB hearing examiner had recommended that the route go to Delta Airlines, a local service outfit in the South. Then by a three-to-two decision, the CAB overruled its examiner (as it does in thirty to forty per cent of all its route cases) and awarded the route to Northeast on August 10, 1956. News of the award leaked and the airline's stock soared on the market.

Northeast's rivals, who considered the Miami route the juiciest plum the CAB would give out for many years, did not yield easily. They fought the decision in the courts, contending that Northeast Airlines was not equipped for the route with planes or pilots. Rumors flew. There were charges of political pressure. Some said, privately but not publicly, that the White House had dictated the decision through the intercession of Sherman Adams, former governor of New Hampshire and then Assistant to President Eisenhower.

The CAB said its decision was based upon its "balanced

route" policy—that is, that every airline should have some profitable long-haul routes to counterbalance the unprofitable but necessary short hauls. The New York–Miami run, primarily a winter operation, would dovetail perfectly with Northeast's slack season, enabling it to improve its New England service. It also promised to relieve the taxpayers of the $2,000,000-a-year subsidy.

The courts upheld the CAB decision and in early December the CAB gave the go-ahead word to Northeast. But to turn a small airline into a big one was a formidable task. Northeast had to acquire more planes, more pilots, more employees all around. It had to lease new terminal space, ticket counter space and maintenance facilities in Florida, and then there was the problem of time. Only two months remained to the 1957 Florida tourist season.

The most pressing problem was to get four-engine equipment before the season ended. In petitioning for the Florida route, Northeast had pointed out that it had ten DC-6Bs on order from Douglas Aircraft. While in 1957 the DC-6Bs were no longer competitive with the newer DC-7s and Lockheed Super Constellations being flown by Eastern Airlines and National Airlines, Northeast had had to hedge when it ordered its ships in 1954. In the event it did not get the Florida route, Northeast planned to use the DC-6Bs to serve its major cities in New England, many of which could not accommodate the larger DC-7s.

However, after it won the route, it learned that it would receive only one DC-6B on January 5, and the next one in March, when the height of the Florida season would have passed.

Searching desperately for four-engine planes, Northeast considered leasing five Constellations from Seaboard and Western Airlines. But to use these planes, Northeast would have had to borrow Seaboard pilots qualified to fly them—and that would have damaged its own line's morale at the start of the new venture. It decided against the Constellations.

Then, late in December, a DC-6A became available. It was a cargo plane converted by the Flying Tiger Line to transport military personnel and dependents between New York and Frankfurt, Germany. The DC-6A was essentially similar to the DC-6B for which the Northeast pilots were being trained. It meant that Northeast could have an extra plane for the latter half of January and all of February.

The plane was not personalized with a provocative name of the kind military aircraft were given during World War II, such as "Lucky Lady" or "Steamy Siren." It was differentiated from other planes merely by its serial number, N 34954.

But while it did not have a name, it did have a carefully recorded history, as do all commercial planes. Every minute of flying time since its manufacture was noted in its own permanent log. The plane's log contained every complaint of a malfunction, every corrective measure of maintenance, every inspection, every overhaul—all were carefully recorded and preserved in the biography of this individual airplane.

Separate records are kept for the airframe, for each engine, each propeller. Overhauls are set for every so many hours on each part of every commercial plane. This is preventive maintenance. Through years of experience, maintenance experts estimate the life span of a given part and each part is changed or overhauled before it reaches its full life expectancy.

Although there is always a double check and, in bigger

airlines, sometimes a triple check of all maintenance work, there is also an increasing application of Murphy's Law in plane construction. Murphy's Law states: "Whatever can be done wrong eventually will be." Murphy's Law therefore requires that, wherever possible, an airplane's parts be so designed that they can be put together only one way: that a plug fit only one socket, that a cable be long enough to reach only the right connection; in short, that it be made impossible for a mechanic to fall into that human error to which he may be prone when servicing an airplane.

By studying N 34954's history, Northeast could see that the Flying Tigers had bought the plane from Douglas Aircraft in January, 1955, that it had been flown sixteen hours before delivery to the Flying Tigers, 3,770 hours by the Flying Tigers in 1955, and 4,266 hours by the Tigers in 1956 for a total of 8,052 hours. Shortly after the Flying Tigers took possession of the plane, they converted it from a freight-carrying configuration to a passenger plane by installing eighty-nine detachable seats. Late in 1956, the Flying Tigers sold the ship to the Main-Elford Corporation, a holding company in Providence, Rhode Island, and then immediately leased the plane back. This was a common arrangement used by airlines to preserve working capital.

The plane, which was available if Northeast wanted to sublease it, had had all its required maintenance overhauls and was certified airworthy. It was ready for use. What's more, the Flying Tigers offered to do all maintenance work on the plane while it was under sublease. This would relieve Northeast of what might become a troublesome task while its own mechanics were brushing up on the new equipment.

While the Flying Tiger plane was only two years old and was certified airworthy, it also was decidedly shabby.

25]

It had a long list of maintenance work and repairs in its log. Its use as a cargo and military personnel carrier, for which good looks did not matter, had not prepared it for the niceties of passenger service.

Leasing the plane was opposed by some of Northeast management. Two of the company's top vice-presidents, Robert Turner, in charge of sales, and Alfred A. Lane, in charge of operations, argued that the reputation of Northeast's new Miami operation might be impaired seriously by a bad first impression on passengers. Reputation was more important in the long run, they said, than immediate financial gain. One shabby plane could ruin Northeast's hopes of attracting the public with its planned luxury flights to Miami. The ten DC-6s on order would have two seats abreast instead of double and triple seats, and each seat would be extra wide and equipped with a folding table for eating and writing. To reduce noise and vibration in the passenger cabin, Northeast had paid for six hundred pounds of added insulation in the wall panels. It would be a mistake to risk the line's reputation by using an unattractive plane at the start, the vice-presidents argued.

But George Gardner, president of Northeast, disagreed. Northeast planned to inaugurate its New York–Miami route on January 20, and it would be next to impossible to operate efficiently with only the one DC-6B. With two planes, it could set up a schedule of at least two round-trip flights daily. And, despite its ragged appearance, the DC-6A represented a potential immediate income of $270,000 for February alone. George Gardner cited the scheduling advantages, the business figures, the needed money to be made this first winter, and he directed Turner to negotiate the lease. Northeast, like most airlines, was run by one man, its president.

Independently wealthy, George Gardner was a rugged individualist with an incisive mind. An old-time pilot, he had flown in the Marine Corps, served in the old Bureau of Air Commerce in the early 1930's; had become vice-president in charge of operations for Northwest Airlines in the late 1930's; left that to become vice-president in charge of operations for National Airlines; and then in the early 1940's had become president of Northeast Airlines.

A trim, five-foot-eight, dynamic boss, George Gardner ruled Northeast Airlines with an iron hand. He was a familiar sight to almost everyone in the airline because he liked to drop in on his employees and find out their problems. No problem on the airline was too small for the president. He liked to make the decisions, all the decisions.

Turner reluctantly arranged to rent the DC-6A from January 1 through March 31 at $112,500 a month. This was not an excessive figure. The Flying Tigers would provide maintenance, repairs, overhaul, spare parts and landing fees, as well as full insurance, including passenger liability coverage of $100,000 per passenger and $9,000,000 per accident. Northeast had only to do the routine turnaround and daily inspection maintenance, for which the Flying Tigers would reimburse it.

The plane was delivered at Idlewild Airport January 1, and Northeast immediately began qualifying pilots in it over the new route. Once the CAB had awarded the five-year "certificate of public convenience and necessity" to fly the Golden Route, Northeast then was obliged to prove to the Civil Aeronautics Administration that it had the airworthy planes and qualified pilots to perform the services it had promised to the CAB.

The federal government's regulation of the aviation industry was divided between the two agencies. The CAB, a small independent agency, had the responsibility of economic regulation of the airlines, including routes, fares and finances, as well as other functions. The much larger CAA, a part of the Commerce Department, enforced the civil air regulations in the day-by-day operations of the airlines, and as part of this function, it certificated planes, crews and various operations of airlines. The CAA was superseded in 1959 by the Federal Aviation Agency.

Thus, before Northeast could begin its new operation, it had to conduct proving flights between New York and Miami to demonstrate to CAA inspectors that its planes, pilots, ground personnel and operating procedures qualified under civil air regulations.

In the rush of these activities, George Gardner, after another dispute with his vice-presidents, made another decision to bring more money into his small company. Instead of starting service on January 20, he moved the inaugural up to January 9. That was nine days after delivery of the DC-6A and only four days after receiving the first DC-6B. Advancing the inaugural date meant that much more money earned. It also meant that much less time to prepare for the vicissitudes of a major airline operation.

The previous month, Northeast had sent seven pilots to the United Airlines Flight Training Center in Denver to be trained for flying a DC-6. The seven were chosen by seniority, for the working conditions and advancement of pilots of all U. S. airlines are ruled by the most rigid seniority system of any business in the country. The system is imposed by the Air Line Pilots Association, which is regarded by many as the strongest single union—vis-à-vis management—in the nation. Some regard it as an association of capitalists rather than a union. Its members earn an average of $16,000 a year piloting piston aircraft and $26,000 to more than $30,000 flying jet airliners.

With a membership of some 13,000 active pilots, who represent about ninety-five per cent of all airline fliers, the union derives its strength from its capacity to halt an airline's operations by striking. An airline is particularly vulnerable because it cannot stockpile service as a steel company stockpiles steel.

Pilots and co-pilots, limited by government regulation to flying no more than eighty-five hours a month, bid monthly for the flight schedules they desire. Seniority alone decides whose bids win. Since a pilot's pay is based on flight time plus type of equipment, with extra pay for night and over-water flying, the senior pilots always bid for the heaviest equipment, the longest flights, the night flights and the shortest turnaround time. More important, whenever a new and usually heavier type of plane is purchased, the senior pilots bid for training to qualify on it.

When jet aircraft came into the market in 1959 and 1960, they had a serious impact upon the seniority system. The jets were a leap, not a jump, above all previous aircraft in weight and speed. They were vastly different in handling. The Federal Aviation Agency, successor to the CAA, at about the same time imposed a mandatory retirement age of sixty upon pilots. This meant that unless the strict seniority system were broken, a pilot fifty-eight or fifty-nine years old could demand jet training—at a cost of $14,000 for flight time alone—and then fly jets only one or two years. As a result, the pilots fought the retirement rule with a vengeance and the airlines fought the seniority system.

The seniority system puts a premium on experience over ability. It assumes that when a man qualifies as a pilot he is as capable as any other pilot and that the longer he flies the better he will be. A pilot himself has no choice, even if he has doubts. The seniority system requires a co-pilot to bid for a captaincy when he becomes senior man in line, even though he may prefer to remain a co-pilot and not assume the responsibility of the left-hand seat in the cockpit.

Although every pilot must pass a proficiency test twice a year, a man may flunk once, twice, thrice, but rarely will he be fired. The union contract forces most airlines simply to train him until he does qualify. This inevitably raises the question: In a real emergency, will this pilot react as he did on the day he passed the test or as he did on the day he flunked it?

Judgment of a pilot's ability is and must be subjective. Some men suffer "checkitis" and become more nervous during a check flight than they do on a scheduled flight. This the check pilot must judge. The Federal Aviation Agency (as was its predecessor, the CAA) is so short of check pilots that the six-month proficiency checks are given by one of several company pilots designated for the task. This puts an extra strain on objectivity because the check pilot then is testing a colleague who often is a personal friend. And, since most men prefer flying regular routes to examining fellow pilots, a check pilot usually takes the job only for the minimum ninety days required. He knows that the man he is testing may be testing him three months later. This situation is more prevalent on the smaller airlines than on larger ones. United Airlines, for instance, maintains a permanent staff of company check pilots at its Denver Center and makes each one a part of management, thus separating the examiner from the line pilot.

This is not to say that any check pilot will endanger lives by passing a grossly inept flier. But that is not the problem. Pilots of commercial airlines are professionals and are not grossly inept. It is a question of how weak must a flier be before he is grounded as dangerous. The number of pilots discharged for poor flying is not often more than two or three per year out of 13,000. Most impartial and informed observers will admit that there are probably more than two or three "weak" men who are flying. But to find them is next to impossible.

The man who can best judge a pilot's ability is his co-pilot, but he is bound by tradition to say nothing critical of his captain. When he does doubt a captain's ability, he usually says nothing but he bids away from that captain by seeking a different flying schedule. When several co-pilots bid away from one man, the airline management can surmise the reason. But even then, many managements seldom can do more than quietly ask the FAA to spot-check the man.

Aside from the seniority system, though, the Air Line Pilots Association vigorously promotes safety. It maintains committees to watch for and report any infraction of government rules by airline managements or airplane manufacturers. Through its member pilots, it is in the best position to spot and report weaknesses in operations which may endanger the public or pilot. It has led the way to guarding against pilot fatigue, overwork or management pressures. While a company may subtly push its pilots to make schedules and to break safety rules if necessary, a pilot always is in a strong position, with his union behind him, to operate his plane in the safest manner he knows.

The seven Northeast pilots sent to Denver each had perhaps fifteen to twenty years' experience, yet they were novices in the DC-6. Every type of plane has different flight and handling characteristics, and for each type the pilot must be trained anew.

No instinct in man is conducive to flying. A pilot must be taught and trained. Each of these seven veterans held the highest airman's qualifications, that of an airline transport pilot. Each had started many years before with a private pilot's license. Each had learned to overcome the first basic problem of flying, to keep the plane in straight and level flight. Each had learned that a plane is basically unstable in the air and tends to fall in a spin or dive unless it is kept under control. While requirements have changed over the years, today a student must have logged thirty-five hours' flying time before getting his private pilot's license.

This first license, now held by some 360,000 men and women in the United States, qualifies a pilot to fly only so long as he can see the ground beneath him and thus tell which side is up. The amateur pilot can easily become disoriented and dive to the earth while his senses tell him he is in straight and level flight. Most airplane accidents each year involve pilots of small aircraft who attempt to fly through bad weather, lose sight of the ground and, because they do not know how to navigate by instruments alone, become disoriented and fly into the ground.

After 200 flying hours in any type plane, a private pilot may take examinations for a commercial pilot's rating, and then for an instrument rating, which requires ten hours of training in flying by instruments alone. This training may be either in a ground simulator or in a plane with a "hooded" cockpit, out of which the student cannot see. Until mid-1960, a flier with these two ratings legally could serve as co-pilot on a modern airliner if he could demonstrate the ability to take off and land the plane. Now these absurdly low requirements have been changed: a co-pilot must demonstrate that he is master of all the navigational and communications procedures required of an airliner captain, and can fly the ship from point of origin to destination himself.

Of course, virtually all airline standards are considerably higher than the legal minimums for co-pilots. Most co-pilots, to retain their jobs, must qualify for the Airline Transport Rating, which every airliner captain must hold.

On most airlines, co-pilots have to work seven to ten years and often more before they move up the seniority list to become captains of a scheduled airliner. Most of today's captains have stuck to flying because they loved it, not because it was an easy way to make a good living. They have known lean years of furlough in slack seasons. They have known what it is like to be a reserve captain, who must stay near his telephone for the call to take out a midnight flight as a substitute for someone else. And, once having become an airline captain, the pilot still must qualify anew on each type of plane he proposes to fly.

He must learn the plane's handling characteristics, its critical speeds for different maneuvers, and he must become thoroughly familiar with its fuel systems, its control systems, its propeller and supercharger operations, its hydraulic system, electric system, anti-icing system, heating, ventilating and pressurization systems. Then he must demonstrate his ability in the normal operations: taxiing, run-up of engines, take-off, climbs and climbing turns, changes of altitude, approaches and landings. This is the normal flying, the easy stuff.

The most important part of his training and of the tests he must pass consists of the emergency maneuvers he may have to use only once in his career. But that once, his life and many other lives will depend on his doing things just right. In these maneuvers, the pilot must demonstrate his ability to make steep turns of at least forty-five degrees without losing more than a hundred feet of altitude. He must fly his plane at just above stalling speed without losing control. He must approach a stall to the point that the plane begins to shudder and buck like an automobile laboring up a hill, and then he must recover control. He must do this not only in level flight but in a turn, and also while coming in for a landing. However, he must never allow the plane actually to stall, for when a plane stalls it loses its lift, its ability to fly, and becomes a mere mass of falling metal.

The pilot must also demonstrate that he can take off with one engine failing at the most critical moment—usually at the end of the runway or below 300 feet altitude. He must show that he can land the plane with two of four engines dead, or, in a twin-engine plane, with one engine failing. He must also show he can maintain both altitude and heading and make moderate turns using only half the plane's power plant.

He must demonstrate as well that he is thoroughly familiar with the characteristics of weather, with navigational and communication facilities, with traffic control procedures, and with the terrain and obstruction hazards of the route which he is to fly. Any pilot can rattle off the altitude of every mountain along his route, and the height of the highest structure near any airport he may use.

The training of a commercial pilot is designed to instill in him a knowledge of and respect for the thousands of rules and regulations in the standard operating procedures manual for his plane, the rules and regulations of the government, and the operating procedures of his own airline.

Above all, the commercial pilot is trained to fly con-

servatively and carefully. This is far more difficult than it
sounds! It means the pilot must submerge his personality,
and even some of his own judgment in flying. It means he
must not push his plane or himself beyond the points set
by his company; in landing, he must execute a missed approach rather than trust himself to descend below airport
minimums—usually 300 feet—before he sees the runway;
he must fly around a cloud at low altitude rather than
through it, lest he hit a mountain peak. Even more important, conservative flying requires that he always be prepared
for the emergency which *might* happen, and he must know
what to do instantaneously. Decisiveness, the ability to
make a decision and make it fast, distinguishes the strong
pilot from the weak one. For a pilot, this decisiveness must
be part of his personality. So must foresight: before take-off,
for instance, the professional pilot assumes that one engine
may fail at a critical moment and he calculates in advance
what corrective action he will take. Before landing, he must
visualize what he will do in the event of engine failure, fire
or gusty cross wind.

But pilots are human and prone to human frailties.
Everyday flying is routine and easy, requiring only a
fraction of a pilot's ability. The tendency is to become
complacent. It is difficult for a man to assume one hundred
times during a flight that his superbly designed plane with
all *its* safeguards may fail him at any moment. So, while
a pilot knows that an emergency may occur, he does not
really believe it will happen this time.

Most flights are routine and routine flying for the professional pilot is as easy as walking a big but well-trained dog.
Some pilots compare flying a plane to having a tiger on a
leash: maintain complete control and the tiger remains
docile; lose control and the tiger can destroy you.

35]

Knowing this, every airline pilot must balance his awareness, or fear, of the potential danger with a relaxed mental attitude. It requires complete self-confidence. Pilots often describe airline flying as ninety-nine per cent boredom and one per cent terror. But awareness of that one per cent can take its toll. The most common occupational ailments of airline pilots are said to be nervous breakdowns and ulcers.

Like all professionals, the pilot has his good days and his bad days. But even at his worst, he must be a safe flier. Never can he drag himself to work with a hangover or fatigue, and this imposes upon him a large measure of self-discipline which rules his personal life twenty-four hours a day. He can hide a hangover from his superiors, but he knows better than to try to hide it from himself. The pilot must keep himself physically fit. Not only must he abstain from alcohol twenty-four hours before going on duty, he also must eat sensibly and be well rested before flying. Most of these practices are required by law or company policy, but pilots and co-pilots adhere to them as a matter of personal integrity and self-protection.

The seven Northeast pilots trained at the United Airlines flight center knew all these rules, and they all passed their written and flight examinations at one of the best flight schools in the country. All obtained rating to fly the DC-6. All were presumably equal in their ability to captain this type of plane safely. How could anyone foretell that one of the seven would crash in a DC-6 in a little more than a month?

Chapter Three

CAPTAIN Alva V. R. Marsh strode into Northeast Airlines' new operations office on the Twentieth Street side of Miami International Airport at about 7:30 on the morning of February 1, 1957. While his passengers were checking in their baggage at the ticket counter, Captain Marsh and his flight crew began to prepare for the first leg of his round-trip flight between Miami and New York.

In appearance he was the prototype of an airline pilot. He was thin and lithe, five feet ten and a half inches tall, weighed 146 pounds, walked erectly with his chin up in the air and he had light brown hair and blue-gray eyes. He wore the powder blue uniform of Northeast Airlines as though it had been tailored for him—as it had been. He exuded the self-assurance of an older, experienced pilot, which, at almost forty-nine years of age, he certainly was.

Born in Montclair, New Jersey, and raised in Baltimore, he had attended Lehigh University for two years. He left school in 1929 to enter an Army flying school in San Antonio, Texas. After learning to fly, he served three years' active duty in the Attack Command in Texas as a reserve second lieutenant-pilot. In 1933, he obtained his first civil pilot's license, flew as co-pilot with Braniff Airways for two months, then quit to seek a regular army commission as a pilot, a prize difficult to win in the depression years. Only sixty of some nine hundred applicants succeeded. He served for some time as an enlisted pilot, still hoping for a commission, and when that did not come through, he joined American Airlines as a co-pilot. He flew a tri-motor Stinson, a low wing ten-passenger plane, and one of the first DC-3s acquired by American Airlines. The DC-3, a milestone in airplane design, was the first fast, reliable twin-engine craft that could fly on one engine in an emergency and carry a profitable payload of twenty-one passengers. It made Douglas Aircraft Company one of the world's leading airplane manufacturers. It was to serve the United States well as the C-47 in World War II, and it was to lead a seemingly unlimited and useful life well into the jet age.

Al Marsh flew as co-pilot with American Airlines for two years, but when he discovered that he probably would have to wait three years more for a captaincy, he accepted an offer that promised more rapid advancement. He joined Northeast in 1938 as a co-pilot and after six months became a captain.

Two years later, when the Yankee Fleet acquired its first DC-3s, with which Al Marsh was familiar, he became chief pilot and trained other Northeast pilots on the plane. One year later, in 1941, he was promoted to operations manager and conducted Northeast's school for training military students in instrument flying in single-engine aircraft. He also trained Northeast crews to ferry planes to England for the Air Transport Command. He tried to reactivate his Army Air Force reserve commission, but the airline insisted he was essential and would not release him.

In 1943, he resigned as operations manager because the job was keeping him from seeing his family more than once in two months, and he returned to active flying, ferrying planes across the Atlantic.

After the end of the war, he resumed commercial flying for Northeast, piloting DC-3s, C-46s, Convair 240s and DC-4s, the first of the four-engine Douglas aircraft.

Al Marsh, in short, was an old-timer. His career progressed with the advance of aviation. His life was flying. He was devoted to the art, and for him it was a full-time occupation. The vast majority of pilots—some estimate it at ninety per cent—develop a second source of income, at some of which they earn as much as they do flying. Several pilots are reputed to be millionaires by dint of their acumen in the stock market. Others are successful real estate brokers, builders, farmers, ranchers, attorneys, businessmen. A pilot's pay is high, leaving him ample money to invest, and his working hours as a pilot are compressed, usually leaving him half of each month for outside activity. But Al Marsh was one of the few pilots who eschewed other employment. He preferred to spend his spare time at home with his lovely, gentle and devoted wife, Ann, and their attractive daughter, Karen. When transferred to the Florida route, Al Marsh moved his family from a Boston suburb to a beautiful home in Miami that had a swimming pool and garden.

To his airline friends Al Marsh was an easygoing man, well liked and respected. He seemed a serene personality— a man of calm, deliberate temperament with a quiet sense of humor and a respect for those around him. By nature, he was soft-spoken and gentle. He was methodical in everything, a trait that is one of the major attributes of a good pilot, and he was known as a good pilot. Yet he was a marked man.

Around each airport that he worked, virtually everyone who flew knew of Al Marsh. He was a rarity. He was the only man, as far as most people could remember, who had cracked up two planes with passengers aboard, and was still flying. Both accidents had occurred within a half mile of one another at La Guardia Airport. Al Marsh had had an unblemished record of sixteen years of safe airline flying when he crashed on January 14, 1952. As captain of a Convair 240 coming in from Boston, he had been checking his co-pilot, Austin E. Briggs, a Convair trainee-captain, in an instrument-approach landing. Visibility that morning had dropped suddenly to half a mile, with a 600-foot ceiling. Captain Marsh called out the descending altitude as the plane came in over water on the back approach to Runway 4, one of the worst airport approaches in the country. When he called out at 500 feet that he had sighted the runway lights, Briggs looked up. Company and government regulations required that a pilot actually see that runway at 500 feet or make a missed approach. Briggs said he could not see the runway. Marsh, as commander, allowed him to continue the descent. The twin-engine plane touched down in Flushing Bay some 3,600 feet short of the runway and sank. The crew of three and the thirty-three passengers aboard escaped death, although five passengers were seriously injured.

The Civil Aeronautics Board, after a ten-month investigation, blamed Al Marsh. "The Board determines that the probable cause of this accident was the failure of the captain in command to monitor the co-pilot's approach and take corrective action when the aircraft first went appreciably below a normal approach path."

Thirteen months later, in the early evening of February 6, 1953, Al Marsh was at the controls, bringing in another Convair 240 from Boston for a landing on Runway 13 of La Guardia Field. Just short of the runway, a hundred feet above ground, the right propeller reversed and the plane yawed sharply to the right. Captain Marsh fought his controls, and brought the plane onto the runway for a crash landing. No one was hurt. The Civil Aeronautics Board attributed the accident to "one of two reasons: namely, malfunction of the right propeller or improper operation of the propeller controls." The Board could go no further. It found nothing wrong mechanically with the propeller or its controls and Al Marsh and his co-pilot vehemently denied applying reverse pitch while the plane was in the air.

"The Board determines that the probable cause of this accident was loss of control of the aircraft during final approach due to high drag from the right propeller. This drag was induced by the right propeller blades moving beyond the high r.p.m. [revolutions per minute] limit stop since the blades were found in approximately zero geometric pitch. The cause of this unwanted propeller action could not be determined."

Pilots as professionals study the findings on each accident for every bit of information that may hold the key to their survival in the future. But what most pilots did not know was that after his second accident, Al Marsh, at his company's suggestion, voluntarily went to one of the nation's leading aviation medical clinics for a complete physical and psychological check-up. The purpose was to determine, if possible, whether he was accident prone and whether any of his traits would point to a predisposition to accidents in other pilots as well.

The search for psychiatric symptoms which might indicate that one man is more accident prone than another has been long, arduous and generally unfruitful. Every pilot undergoes psychiatric tests before he is hired by an airline, but the tests can only roughly gauge a man's personality.

Al Marsh was given a clean bill of mental health after his second accident. There was nothing in any test administered by the clinic to indicate he was in any way accident prone. Still, the hierarchy of Northeast argued over Al Marsh's continuing to fly. To some, two accidents spelled accident proneness, per se. To others, the two accidents were chance misfortunes. Northeast President Gardner decided to stick with Al Marsh and Marsh returned to flying as the fourth ranking pilot in seniority on the airline.

Between his first flight over the new route on January 10 and this February 1, Al Marsh had made ten trips between New York and Miami, all in the same DC-6A. This, plus his training flights, added up to some sixty-five hours' flying time in that one plane and another fifteen hours or so in the DC-6B in which he had been trained in Denver. So, while he had amassed some 18,000 hours' flying time over nineteen years, he was still considered a new man in a DC-6. The industry's rule of thumb is that the first one hundred pilot hours in any new equipment are critical for the pilot-in-command. Take-off and landing minimums usually are raised during those first one hundred hours. Some airlines assign supervisory pilots to their jet planes being flown by pilots with fewer than one hundred hours' jet flying time.

But such precautions usually entail the spending of money which cuts into profits, and Northeast Airlines did not have the financial avoirdupois to spare. It planned to have its seven qualified DC-6 pilots train other men on the line, thus saving the money it would cost to put more men through the United Airlines Training School.

Captain Marsh's co-pilot for the round-trip flight was Basil S. Dixwell, another old-timer on the airline but a newcomer to the DC-6. Dixwell, a tall, well-built man who wore glasses, was forty years old. In aviation since 1939, he had become a co-pilot for Northeast in January, 1942, and a year later a captain, qualifying over the years in each of the Northeast planes: the DC-3, CW-20, Convair 240 and DC-4. Like Captain Marsh, he had once been chief pilot of Northeast Airlines, but, like many other chief pilots throughout the country, he had abandoned the prestige job, which demanded long hours of desk work, to return to regular flying.

Basil Dixwell had attended about sixty-five hours of ground-school classes on the DC-6, conducted by Northeast Airlines in East Boston in January. He had flown several trips to Miami as an observer in the cockpit, and had made his required three take-offs and landings under the guidance of a qualified pilot. Then, in February, he was assigned as co-pilot to Captain Marsh as part of his training for the day when he would take his qualification test for a DC-6 captaincy. In personality, Basil Dixwell was far more the extrovert than Marsh. He was outspoken, sure of himself, and had a wide range of interests beyond aviation. His second job was raising purebred Angus and Hereford cattle in Stratham, New Hampshire, where he lived.

Captain Marsh and Dixwell together planned their flight to New York. They checked the weather and winds en route. They chose Idlewild Airport as an alternative landing place in the event that La Guardia were closed in by weather. They computed that the usual 3,000 gallons of gasoline would take them to Idlewild and provide an extra forty-five minutes of flying time as a safety margin. With existing tail winds, Marsh calculated he would make it to La Guardia in just about the scheduled time. All Northeast flights between New York and Miami were scheduled for four hours so that one crew could complete the round trip within the legal limit of eight hours' scheduled flying time in one day. While it was not impossible, it would be a rare day indeed when any DC-6 could make the round trip in eight hours' flying time.

All airline flying in the "golden triangle" of New York –Chicago–Miami must be done according to instrument-flight rules; that is, every airliner must fly an exact prescribed course along existing flight paths that run like highways in the sky. The plane checks in at each control point along the route, and the control centers keep track of the position of every plane above 9,500 feet, where the airliners fly. Thus, traffic controllers help pilots maintain a safe separation between airliners in the crowded skies.

The preferred instrument routing from Miami to New York is via Control 1150 Airway, which takes a plane from Miami to Palm Beach and out over the Atlantic in a straight line to Wilmington, North Carolina, and thence northward over land to New York. This route is the straightest and shortest, and hence the cheapest. It costs an estimated $5 a minute to fly a DC-6 (and about five times as much to fly a jet airliner), and every minute saved is a minute earned.

Captain Marsh noted that this day there was some missile activity posted for the Cape Canaveral area and that a section of Control 1150 Airway was closed to air traffic. He still could fly up the coast beyond Cape Canaveral, cut out over the Atlantic to Baracuta, a check point on the airway, and then follow 1150 to Wilmington. But that would entail some difficult radio navigation and inexact dead reckoning because of winds and tricky radio reception far out at sea.

Instead, he chose the overland route, Victor 3 and Victor 1, and he left it to Dixwell to do the detail work of setting down the required check points and the radio frequencies involved for communications en route. Dixwell figured the route up the coast from Miami to West Palm Beach to Vero Beach, Daytona Beach, Jacksonville, Brunswick (Georgia), Savannah, Charleston (South Carolina), Myrtle Beach (South Carolina), Wilmington (North Carolina), and then the regular overland route to New York via Norfolk (Virginia), Salisbury (Maryland), Atlantic City (New Jersey), and La Guardia Airport.

While Dixwell worked out the flight plan, and gave it to the company dispatcher to file with the control tower, Captain Marsh conferred with his maintenance department. He had brought the plane in at 6:45 the previous morning from a night round-trip flight to New York. Another pilot had taken the plane out later that morning for another round trip to New York, but he had returned to Miami Airport shortly after take-off with the complaint that the No. 1 propeller had over-revved and could not be controlled. The flight had been canceled.

Maintenance informed Captain Marsh that the plane had been taken up early that morning and all items on the previous pilot's squawk list had been checked off, with one exception. The correct size cams, which controlled the speed of the No. 1 propeller, were not available in Miami but would be installed when the plane reached La Guardia. The Flying Tiger man who was responsible for the maintenance of the plane in Miami declared the plane airworthy, and Captain Marsh, having no reason to doubt him, accepted the plane.

Meanwhile, the third member of the flight crew had inspected the plane thoroughly and had set the controls and electrical circuits in preparation for the flight. He was the flight engineer, Angelo Andon, a man just one month shy of thirty-four years, who had been one of fourteen hangar mechanics of Northeast lucky enough to be chosen for flight engineer school when the Miami route was awarded to Northeast. Without the Miami route Andon, who had spent some thirteen years in aviation, would not have had a hope of achieving flying status. Twin-engine planes used by the airline in New England did not require flight engineers. But with the new route, the pilots' union persuaded Northeast to make the third man in their DC-6 cockpit a pilot-qualified engineer who would be a member of ALPA rather than an engineer who would be a member of the Flight Engineers Association. So, Andon and thirteen others were put on the all-important pilots' seniority list, which meant that eventually they would become eligible for pilot training and possible captaincies. Andon and his colleagues attended the flight engineer training school of National Airlines, because Northeast at the time had neither flight engineers nor a school to train them. By February 1, Andon had made about six round trips between Miami and New York, two of them with Captain Marsh, none with Dixwell. He had sixty hours' flying experience, all in a DC-6.

As flight engineer, Andon arrived at the airport shortly before 7:30 A.M. and began giving the DC-6A, standing before the loading gate, a complete inspection. Although it is the captain who has the ultimate responsibility for deciding whether or not a plane is airworthy, it is his flight engineer who is his principal adviser on the subject. Andon, with awareness of this responsibility, made a careful, walk-around inspection of the plane, as does the flight engineer of every airliner before take-off. It was a visual inspection to note any dents, loose ends or anything which might endanger the flight. Inside the plane, he inspected first the passenger cabin, the emergency exits, and then, in the cockpit, he went through a long routine of switching on the multitudinous electrical circuits and radio receivers and transmitters.

Andon also reviewed the pilot squawk list of the previous flight and checked with Frank Robinson, the Flying Tiger maintenance man, that the plane was airworthy and ready to go.

Only after Captain Marsh and First Officer Dixwell entered the cockpit, and Andon reported to the captain that the plane was ready to go, did the first passengers begin boarding.

The plane itself, freshly painted in the Northeast colors of white with blue horizontal stripes on the fuselage and tail, stood stolidly before the loading gate, 105 feet long, 117 feet 6 inches broad from wingtip to wingtip. Its rudder stood 28 feet 8 inches high in the clear Florida air. Aloft, it was graceful; on the ground it looked like a squat monster. Yet, the DC-6 was in fact one of the finest airplanes ever designed. It was to the aviation industry in the early postwar years after 1947 what the Boeing 707 and DC-8 jet were to transportation in 1959: the herald of a new age of air travel. The DC-6 had double the passenger capacity and speed of prewar airliners. More important, it and the Lockheed Constellation were the first of the large pressurized cabin planes. The pressurized cabin allowed the aircraft to cruise at altitudes above 10,000 feet, where

47]

the air was thin and the plane could go faster on less fuel. Most important, it was a moneymaker. For the airlines, the DC-6 meant they could run a plane half empty and still make a profit. To pilots, the DC-6 was a work horse, a plane which might handle like a truck, but was reliable and safe. Over the years, the DC-6 would prove itself to be the most popular piston airliner, carrying more passengers than any other plane in the world.

Up to the advent of the jets, the DC-6 and the triple-tail Constellation were the bulwarks of American aviation. Yet both planes had had their troubles early in life. All DC-6s were grounded for about eight months in 1947 while investigators sought the reason why three DC-6s had caught fire aloft and crashed in flames. The cause turned out to be a bit of bad plumbing in a magnificent plane. A wing fuel-tank vent was discovered to have been so positioned that when excess fuel spewed through the vent, it traveled along the underbelly of the plane into the air scoop of the cabin heater farther aft. The combination of high-octane gasoline and heat was enough to send any plane crashing in flames. Once the cause was known, the cure was simple. The position of the heater air intake was changed.

In the Lockheed Constellation, which was grounded for a month in late 1946 because of a series of fires in flight, the trouble turned out to be a bad job of electrical work in six small bolts, which brought electrical power from the generators in the wings into the pressurized cabin. The bolts, known as through-studs, had been working loose, rubbing against the metal fuselage and creating enough electrical arcing to set fire to a nearby hydraulic line, which had a tendency to leak flammable hydraulic fluid. The cure was simple. The design and installation of the through-stud bolts were improved, the hydraulic lines were moved farther away, a nonflammable fluid was substituted and a better fire-detection system was added to the cockpit.

Ten years later, all such "bugs" had long been eliminated from both the Constellation and the DC-6. Still, any mechanical trouble with either plane or, for that matter, any airliner, had to be reported to the CAA in a "daily mechanical report," which encompasses every mechanical or operational difficulty encountered on the previous day. In the offices of both the CAA and CAB, analysts review these reports daily to find trends. Thus, the faulty landing gear of the Boeing 707 was redesigned before a single life was lost in an accident. Thus, the plate glass in the windshields of early DC-8 jets, which cracked under certain pressures, was changed before the public even became aware of the difficulty which might one day have caused a disaster.

The cockpit of an airliner, so complex and awesome to the layman, is the business office of the professional pilot. It is small and crowded. Buttons, switches, levers, wheels, dials, gauges, fill the panel in front of the pilot; they cover the space above the windshield and stretch along the ceiling; they run down the side of the plane, and they dot the knee-high pedestal between the pilot and co-pilot.

The only comfort in the DC-6 cockpit is provided by the cushioned armchairs for the pilot and co-pilot. The flight engineer is relegated to a mere jump seat, not much more than an upholstered board, which fits down over the aisle between the two pilots.

With his flight engineer at his right shoulder and his co-pilot in the right-hand seat beside him, Captain Marsh began the ritual of the pre-take-off check list which is designed to insure the maximum degree of safety. The check-list procedure, putting a premium on attention to detail, makes modern airline flying a cut-and-dried business most of the time, but it is largely responsible for the safety statistics.

Al Marsh had no argument with this conservative approach to flying. Following the steps on the check list, he smoothly taxied the plane away from the Northeast loading gate at 8:46, a minute behind schedule. At the head of the runway, he received final clearance, revved his four engines and flipped off the brakes. The plane roared down the runway and at 8:56 A.M. it rose slowly into the air.

The take-off was as routine and normal as any of the five hundred to six hundred take-offs from Miami Airport on an average day in February. The No. 1 engine again went to 2,900 revolutions per minute. Each of the three men in the cockpit at least once toggled the small lever which brought the r.p.m. down to the desired 2,800, and each kept close watch on that engine. Actually, it was a minor matter. The added 100 r.p.m. put No. 1 engine out of synchronization with the other three, but one would know it only by observing the tachometer.

As the engine was brought into control, Captain Marsh climbed to his assigned altitude of 19,000 feet, leveled off and headed for his first check point at West Palm Beach. At cruising altitude, he could relax.

Flying a DC-6 is like driving a heavy truck: it involves a good deal of manual work. But electronics have provided airplanes with the automatic pilot, and once he had trimmed the plane on its proper course, Captain Marsh engaged the autopilot and let it do the manual work. Tuning the VOR radio to his next check point, he engaged three levers of the automatic pilot on the pedestal next to him: one controlled the ailerons to bank and turn the plane, the second controlled the elevators on the tail stabilizers for up and down movement, and the third controlled the rudder which stabilized turns. With Captain Marsh's desired heading set on his VOR instrument, the autopilot guided the plane on course, compensating for any pitching and rolling.

Thus, the plane was flown by instruments and the two pilots had no need to look out their windows except to admire the view at 19,000 feet. The view happened to be grand. Clouds were scattered and one could see the earth almost four miles below.

At West Palm Beach, the first check point, First Officer Dixwell reported in, giving the plane's position, the time, altitude and estimated time of arrival at the next check point. Then he identified the check point after next, so that there would be no mistake about the plane's route at the air route control center. Thus, he reported something like this: "Northeast 822, over West Palm Beach at 0855 at 19,000; Vero Beach at 0905; then Daytona."

In the cockpit, there was the usual amount of paper work. Dixwell computed ground speed by measuring time against the known distance in miles between check points. Flight Engineer Andon kept the "howgozit" chart, constantly computing the amount of gasoline used and the amount remaining. Captain Marsh, with the help of his autopilot, flew in a state of relaxed tension sought by the perfect pilot, a condition in which the nerves are relaxed but the whole being is alert for any vicissitude. Cruising through a bright and calm sky at 19,000, the engines purring in sychronization, Captain Marsh had only to guard against a state of mind known to pilots as Fat, Dumb and Happy.

Many pilots have gone to their deaths while flying Fat,

Dumb and Happy. Student fliers happily awed with handling a plane have flown straight into the ground unaware of what was happening. Young commercial pilots so intent upon following the glide path for a perfect instrument landing that they forget to lower the landing gear—they were Fat, Dumb and Happy. It can happen to veteran captains too. The transport pilot whose mind wanders as he expertly noses his plane down from one assigned altitude to another and then forgetfully continues to descend—he is Fat, Dumb and Happy, at least until his co-pilot judiciously taps his shoulder and points to the altimeter. No pilot, whether he is master of a jet airliner or of a Piper Cub, can afford the absent-mindedness that the man on the ground may enjoy without danger.

Approaching La Guardia Field less than four hours after take-off from Miami, Northeast Flight 822 was cleared by the La Guardia Tower for a straight-in approach. The first wisps of fog had set in earlier that morning in New York and a few minutes after noon, the first snow flurries began. One of the advantages of bad flying weather is that it keeps most of the small private planes on the ground, cutting delays for airliners in landing or taking off from the usually jammed airports. The sky over the United States is used by some 2,000 airliners, 30,000 military craft and 69,000 privately owned planes. It is a crowded sky, particularly around airports, where precision patterns of flying are prescribed for all planes taking off or coming in for a landing. The awesome mid-air collision is without doubt the most feared aspect of flying for airline pilots. On June 30, 1956, a United Airlines DC-7 and a Trans World Airlines Constellation collided over the Grand Canyon and everyone aboard both planes perished. With 128 casualties, it was the worst commercial plane disaster in history until December 16, 1960. On that day, ironically, a United DC-8 jet, coming into Idlewild Airport, and a TWA Constellation, approaching La Guardia Airport, collided over New York City, resulting in the death of 128 passengers and six people on the ground.

With the same ritual observance of the check list that he had followed at take-off, Captain Marsh and his crew prepared for the descent at La Guardia. Landings account for the majority of all mishaps. It is a delicate operation to set upon the earth 100,000 pounds of airplane hurtling along at 130 or more miles per hour. Al Marsh himself had crashed twice landing at this very airport. The three-man crew carefully checked all engine readings, and switched on the heat for the carburetors, the wings, the tail section, the propellers and the pitot tubes, all of which had to be kept free of icing to insure a safe landing. They computed the plane's landing weight by subtracting the amount of gasoline, at six pounds per gallon, used during the flight, and then established the required speed for landing that weight without stalling.

Descending steadily from 19,000 feet, the airliner encountered a cloud bank over the airport at about 6,000 feet. Captain Marsh then went on instruments, guiding the plane into the field manually by radio. The barometric pressure was obtained from the airport and the plane's altimeter calibrated accordingly. The fuel mixture was boosted to auto-rich, the hydraulic system was checked, the landing gear lowered and locked in place. The NO SMOKING—FASTEN SEAT BELTS sign was flashed on in the passenger cabin. Captain Marsh brought the big plane in on the glide path of his instrument landing system. Two needles on a single gauge told him when his plane was too

high, too low, too far to the right, or too far to the left of
the one path which would set him down on Runway 22.
Outside, one could see only opaque grayish-white clouds.
But Captain Marsh did not look outside. He was intent on
his instruments, until Dixwell called out that he could see
the runway lights. The altitude was 800 feet, well above
the required minimum. Al Marsh then, and only then,
looked up and out his forward windshield. He too espied
the runway lights. The remainder of the landing would be
visual. As his co-pilot called out each hundred feet of less-
ened altitude, Captain Marsh brought the plane down in
line with the runway lights.

Chapter Four

WITH wing flaps full down and his co-pilot calling out the speed and altitude, Captain Marsh eased back on the four throttles to reduce speed, gently pulled back on his control wheel to keep the nose up, and manipulated both hand and foot controls to keep the plane aligned with the runway.

Landing a plane is like lining up a fifteen-foot putt in tournament golf. It takes perfect co-ordination and consideration of all possible contingencies. There could be the sudden gust of cross wind to twist the ship, the unexpected patch of fog to obscure the runway at a crucial moment, the downdraft which drops the plane fifty or a hundred feet. There can be an engine failure, an electrical failure which short-circuits a vital instrument. . . .

But the delicacy and danger of an instrument landing are precisely the elements which give the professional pilot pride in his work. In a well-executed landing, the wheels touch down with so little pressure that passengers hardly discern the difference between flying and racing down the runway. Such a landing brings joy to a pilot's heart.

Captain Marsh touched down at 12:51 P.M., completing his 1,092-mile flight from Miami. He taxied to Northeast's Gate 11, where his passengers, tanned and glowing from the Florida sun, disembarked at 1 P.M, into a foul, gray winter day. Wet, gray fog had descended upon the airport and a thin layer of snow already covered the ground.

Captain Marsh and Dixwell strode into the Northeast operations room for a few minutes of routine paper work. Then they went to the Kitty Hawk restaurant on the second floor of the main terminal building for a quick lunch before planning their flight back to Miami. Flight 823 was scheduled to take off at 2:45 P.M.

Their plane stood outside Gate 11. The snowfall was now heavy. Andon, the flight engineer, stayed with the plane to complete his preflight check for the return trip before he went to lunch. He had 234 individual items to inspect and it took him the better part of an hour. There was the walk-around inspection to see if any part of the fuselage, the wings or empennage had been damaged on the way north. Inside the passenger cabin, there were 38 items to be scrutinized, including doors, windows, emergency exits, lights, switches and electrical circuits. In the cockpit there were 68 switches, buttons and controls to set.

At the same time, the ground crews went to work. Three mechanics refueled the wing tanks with 1,673 gallons of 100-octane gasoline, bringing the supply back up to the required 3,000 gallons. The plane was serviced with 23 gallons of lubricating oil. The hydraulic system, the superchargers, the alcohol tanks, were checked. The engines were given an "in transit" inspection and found to be all right.

John Joy, acting lead mechanic of the ground crew, examined the plane's log and found it free of pilot squawks. The maintenance department did have a teletype message from the Northeast dispatcher in Miami saying that the high-frequency radio receiver should be checked because Flight 822 when airborne had not heard Northeast's radio in Miami. The airline's electrician, engineer and a mechanic checked the receiver and could find nothing wrong. But since they did not have the time to check with the pilot, who was eating, the electrician changed the receiver.

At the same time, maintenance men from the Flying Tiger Line went over the No. 1 propeller, but they could not find the right-sized governor to correct the slight over-revving.

Neither the radio receiver nor over-revving engine complaint was recorded on the plane's log—a violation of civil air regulations which was minor but would not be tolerated on most airlines. Only by recording every malfunction, minor or not, can a useful history of a plane be maintained.

The flight log, which is supposed to be removed from the plane at the end of each trip, was forgotten aboard by John Joy, who had become busy with other things. The logs containing pilot complaints dating back to January 28 also were left aboard, contrary to civil air regulations.

While the ground crews worked on the plane out in the snow—because Northeast did not have its own hangar at La Guardia—Captain Marsh and his co-pilot, eating lunch, were observed with interest by some of the passengers waiting for Flight 823. Among those who recognized the Northeast uniforms was Gerry Lassell, the instrument mechanic from Boston, who sat near the restaurant's picture window facing the apron of the airport. Lassell, looking at the DC-6 in the snow, worried not about the weather but about his chances of getting a ride on the afternoon flight. Lassell, his wife and small son were among thirteen of Northeast's people who had been bumped off the DC-6B morning flight from Boston by passengers who boarded at New York. Now the thirteen were stand-bys for the afternoon flight. Their only hope of getting to Florida that day was that Flight 823 would not fill up with paying customers. Dorothy Richardson, her husband and son had not been bumped because she was traveling on a business pass in connection with the Miami training program for stewardesses. Her father, mother and sister had to leave the plane at La Guardia like the others with family passes.

Among the couples bumped, Mary and Arthur Bourgoin, who lived on an airline ticket agent's salary in Maine, were so appalled by the prices on the Kitty Hawk menu that they looked their waiter square in the eye and ordered the cheapest sandwich. In the Kitty Hawk restaurant, as in its counterparts in airports across the country, the diner pays for a glorious view as well as the food (which usually is far less than glorious). The restaurant's picture window provided a panorama of the airport's taxiway and apron, where one could see the coming and going of sleek airships, a spectacle comparable to the beauty of the harbor of a seaside resort.

The Kitty Hawk restaurant may well be said to be the only attractive thing about La Guardia Airport, and even the beauty of the restaurant itself is open to question. Nevertheless, La Guardia Airport is one of the most important airfields in the country. Situated in northwestern Queens County, only eight miles from New York's Times Square, and bordering on Flushing Bay and Bowery Bay, the airport was built on muck, mire and a thousand mistakes. Yet its construction was a considerable and foresighted achievement. It was New York City's first commercial airport, and it was the nation's first self-contained "airport city" with its own shopping area, bank, restaurants and other commercial enterprises. Its construction can be credited almost solely to one man, New York's melodramatic mayor, Fiorello H. La Guardia, who had been a pilot in World War I. He dramatized the start of his fight for federal funds for an airport for New York in 1934. Newark (N.J.) Municipal Airport then was the only mail and passenger field for the nation's largest city. On the night of November 24, 1934, the short, pudgy Fiorello La Guardia refused to follow nine other passengers out of a TWA plane which landed at Newark Airport. He insisted his plane ticket read "Chicago–New York" and he wanted to be flown to New York. Since he refused to budge (and since the newspapers had been alerted), TWA yielded and flew him, the first air passenger from the West to land in New York, to Floyd Bennett Field in Brooklyn. He continued his fight through the depression years and in 1937, Works Progress Administration men broke ground for what was to become La Guardia Airport.

Some five thousand men worked three shifts a day, six days a week for almost two years. The original cost estimate of $13 million rose to $40 million, and the original 105 acres of what had once been an amusement park and then a small private airstrip were transformed into a 558-acre modern airport. It was done by filling in the marshes of Flushing Bay with millions of tons of ashes, cinders and rubbish from what in those days was a city dump on nearby Rikers Island. Dedication ceremonies were held in October, 1939, a month after the second World War had begun, and on December 2, 1939, the airport was opened to commercial aviation. Then La Guardia Airport's troubles really began.

The field began to sink and it continued to sink for twenty years. The weight of its buildings, runways and planes compressed the muck below and the muck oozed out into Flushing Bay. The main terminal building had to be reinforced by hydraulic jacks lest its first floor sink out of sight. The runways, which made roller-coaster rides of landings and take-offs, had to be repaved again and again.

Yet as more people accepted commercial aviation, La Guardia Airport became more and more important, and more and more money was poured into it. The Port of New York Authority, an independent agency which took over the operation of the airport in 1947, spent $16 million over the next twelve years in keeping the field up to date. Finally, in 1959, the Port Authority announced a full-scale program to reconstruct the airport at an estimated cost of $56 million, approximately the same amount that had been spent on La Guardia Airport since its completion in 1939.

Lest anyone think this extravagant, the Port Authority can point to the tremendous growth of aviation needs. Since 1948, when the much larger Idlewild Airport was built on the opposite shore of Long Island in the expectation that it would *replace* La Guardia, the air traffic at La Guardia Airport has almost doubled. In 1948, for instance, there were 145,444 landings and take-offs at La Guardia. In 1957, despite the full operation of nearby Idlewild Airport, there were 245,340 plane movements at La Guardia.

So, on the first day of February, 1957, the long narrow corridor of airline ticket counters was abuzz with activity. No matter the weather or the time of day, La Guardia Airport is always crowded with passengers, relatives and well-wishers. In 1957, it ranked second among the nation's airports in the number of airliners landing and taking off. It ranked sixth in the number of all types of aircraft movements in and out of the airport. Averaged out around the clock, a plane lands or takes off from La Guardia Airport every two minutes every day of the year. Actually, in the daylight and early evening hours, a plane lands or takes off every minute; often the time between planes is less than a full minute.

After a half-hour lunch, Captain Marsh and his co-pilot made their way through the crowds to the Northeast operations office at 1:45 P.M. The release for Flight 823 from the company's flight superintendent, or dispatcher, already was at the operations office.

The airline, peculiarly, had chosen to station dispatchers for the New York–Miami operation in Miami rather than New York. Most airlines have dispatchers at both ends of an important route so that a dispatcher, who represents the company in the decisions affecting the safety of the flight, may be on the scene to determine weather conditions, the airworthiness of the plane and other factors affecting the flight. However, the Miami and New York operations offices of Northeast could maintain constant communication, and the dispatcher in Miami had the same U. S. Weather Bureau information concerning La Guardia that he would have had in New York.

Captain Marsh read the flight release which had been teletyped to New York: RELEASE FLT 823 LGA MIA VIA AWYS INST AUTHO ALT PBI DEPT LGA 18.000 LBS FUEL IFR ATC MAX GROSS DEPT LGA 97.275 TO RNWY 4 MATTHEWS MIAO 011300

Translated this meant: "Release Flight 823 La Guardia–Miami via airways. Instruments authorized. Alternate landing at West Palm Beach. Departing La Guardia with 18,000 pounds fuel. Instrument flight rules under Air Traffic Control. Maximum gross weight departing La Guardia 97,275 pounds. Take-off Runway 4. (signed) Matthews, Miami Operations, February 1, at 1 P.M."

Robert Matthews, who had dispatched the DC-6A on its northbound flight from Miami that morning, had begun preparing his release for the return flight even before the plane had landed at La Guardia. He based his release primarily upon the U. S. Weather Bureau's 12:30 P.M. report on existing conditions at La Guardia. All the weather information he needed was contained in one line of shorthand hieroglyphics:

LGA 1230E WX 150M2005S - - 34/29 11/016 SB 02 QURUA 4-22

Translated, this said: "La Guardia 12:30 P.M. Eastern Standard Time, Weather: scattered clouds at 1,500 feet— measured broken deck of clouds at 2,000 feet—five miles visibility with very light snow. Temperature 34, dew point 29. Wind, northeast 11 knots. Barometric pressure 30.16 inches. Snow began at 12:02 P.M.—Runway 4-22 closed."

With this information, the flight superintendent knew that the weather was far above the Northeast minimums of 200-foot ceiling and one-quarter-mile visibility for the take-off of a four-engine airplane at La Guardia. He calculated the maximum allowable gross weight for Flight 823's take-off from Runway 4. The runway was long enough to provide a safe take-off for a 94,000-pound plane on a day when there was no wind and the temperature was 59 degrees. For every knot of head wind, 190 pounds could be added to the allowable weight of the plane, and for every degree below 59 another fifty-five pounds could be added. The Northeast dispatcher, figuring roughly for ten instead of eleven knots of head wind, added 1,900 pounds to the basic weight for the wind and 1,375 pounds for the temperature, and computed the maximum allowable take-off weight for Flight 823 to be 97,275 pounds.

The note that Runway 4, the only instrument runway at La Guardia, was closed did not worry the dispatcher. He knew it was closed to permit repairs to the dike at the Flushing Bay end of the runway and if the weather deteriorated further, the instrument runway would be opened.

In the La Guardia operations office, Captain Marsh read the release carefully, for it was up to him as pilot to agree or disagree with the dispatcher. He could reject the release and say the weather was not suitable for flying. The latest weather-sequence report, made at 1:30 P.M., showed a marked drop in visibility.

Precipitation ceiling at 1,000 feet, obscuration 5/8ths of a mile, light snow, haze, smoke. Temperature 32, dew point 31. Wind northeast 9 knots. Barometric pressure 30.14. Visibility 5/8ths of a mile on Runway 4, the 1:30 P.M. weather report read.

The ceiling had fallen 500 feet and was closing in. The temperature and dew point, drawing together, indicated the air was almost one hundred per cent saturated with moisture. The barometric pressure was falling, and most important, the visibility was barely above the legal limit for take-off.

Northeast's minimum weather requirements for take-off from La Guardia were the same as those of the airport itself: 200-foot ceiling and one-quarter-mile visibility. The airport's minimums were absolute minimums, below which it would be unsafe to attempt a take-off. All of the bad weather, however, was at La Guardia. Captain Marsh, studying the weather en route, could see that once he climbed above the rain and snow, he would be in the clear.

He would be flying south, away from the bad weather to the sunshine of Florida and to the warmth of his own family and home. Since the flight superintendent was in Miami and not in New York, there was no one for the pilot to consult; the decision was for Marsh to make. His job was to fly in good weather and bad, as long as the weather was above legal minimums and he believed the flight could be made safely. The weather was just about as bad as it could get and remain flyable. With the temperature hovering at the freezing point and so close to the dew point, it meant that he would have heavy, wet snow clinging to his plane and that ice might form on his wings. He would have preferred either lower temperatures which would have brought snow too cold to stick to his plane or higher temperatures which would have meant rain.

To the layman, the weather looked terrible. To the airman, it was marginal, not so bad that four-engine airliners could not be flown in it. Some pilots canceled, some flew. Marsh decided to fly.

He asked a Flying Tiger maintenance man, who was warming himself by a radiator in the office, whether repairs to the No. 1 propeller would cause any delay in take-off. The mechanic replied there would be no delay, explaining that the maintenance men could not find the right-sized governors to keep the prop from over-revving, but it had been fixed so that the plane could take off.

Marsh was not too concerned about this, for even if the propeller continued to shoot 100 r.p.m. over the other three, it would not affect the plane's flying characteristics.

The captain left his plan for the flight to Miami with an operations man to pass on to the control tower, and at about 2:25 P.M. he and his crew went out into the snow and boarded the waiting DC-6A.

[64

When Captain Marsh and his first officer climbed into the cockpit to join the flight engineer, the ground crew men were sweeping snow off the plane. The ground crew was beleaguered with work. Besides the Miami flight, there were two DC-3s and one Convair which had to be cleaned of snow. C. E. Cruickshank, the Northeast station manager at La Guardia, told lead mechanic John Joy to hold over his morning crew for overtime work. Joy estimated it would take at least a half hour to get the snow off the DC-6, and Cruickshank relayed the information to the Northeast chief ticket agent to delay the boarding of passengers.

Many passengers had already checked their baggage and were lining up at Gate 11. The nonrevenue passengers who were stand-bys crowded about the ticket counter, discussing the weather and their chances of getting aboard the plane. Paying passengers also talked about the weather and whether or not to fly.

Hyman Schwartz, a fifty-two-year-old Brooklyn attorney, again and again changed his mind. It was his first flight and he was to join his wife, who had motored to Miami Beach with relatives a week before. "If you're so nervous, you can always cancel," suggested his son, Joel, a twenty-three-year-old senior at Brooklyn College. "No, I might as well go . . . as long as I'm out here," said the elder Mr. Schwartz.

For those who had flown down to New York from New England a change of mind would involve the discomfort of being stranded in New York. Mrs. Chopelas, who had already spent more than three hours waiting at the airport, tried to appease her tired, fidgety and whining young son by buying him a large $6 model of a DC-6.

In the cockpit of the DC-6A, Captain Marsh and Dixwell set up and tuned the various radios. The plane, like all airliners, carried close to a hundred thousand dollars' worth of radio equipment, including two very high-frequency (VHF) transmitters and receivers and two low-frequency (ADF) receivers for navigation and two VHF communications transmitters and receivers for standard air-to-ground contact, plus one high-frequency transmitter and receiver for contact with the company operations office.

Captain Marsh, preferring to navigate out of La Guardia with his low-frequency radios, set one ADF (automatic direction finder) radio to the frequency of the range station at Clasons Point in the Bronx. The radio range station was 2.8 miles directly ahead of the end of Runway 4. Thus he could maintain his direction straight away from the runway by keeping that ADF needle on his instrument panel pointing straight up. The other low-frequency radio he tuned to the Paterson, New Jersey, range station, so that when he flew over Clasons Point and the first needle fell away, he could follow the second needle pointing to the Paterson station. For the third leg of his flight, he set one of the VHF radios to the omnirange station at Caldwell, New Jersey.

By setting up three radios in advance, the pilot could then direct his attention solely to flying. Although Captain Marsh was relying on his low-frequency navigational radios, the trend in modern aviation is toward the high-frequency facilities, which are not affected by atmospheric electricity prevalent in storms. Low-frequency receivers, much like home radios, are affected by static and are less accurate.

While making last-minute cockpit preparations, Captain Marsh observed through his side window the activity of the men removing snow from the left wing. Two men atop the wing swept the snow down toward the trailing, or back, edge of the wing, and from the ground a third man, Pete Tsantes, reached up with a broom and pulled the snow to the ground. But as the men swept the expanse of wing, more snow fell.

At 2:40 P.M., Gate 11 was opened and passengers gingerly made their way toward the open main door of the cabin. The loading agent at the gate took each ticket and checked his list of passengers.

The passengers, most of them laden with heavy coats, as well as bags full of paraphernalia for a vacation in the sun, hunched their shoulders against the cold. At the door they were greeted warmly by Doris Steele, the senior stewardess. Because of a mix-up in reservations, some people began disputing over seats, and the two other stewardesses, Kay Virchow and Emily Gately, tried to clear up the confusion while leading the passengers to their places.

An aura of pleasant excitement filled the plane: passengers anticipated their escape from New York's weather and even the stewardesses looked forward to this trip. Dottie Steele pointed out to the two younger stewardesses that this was one of Northeast's first full loads to Miami since the route's start, auguring success for the company. Devoted to Northeast, she communicated her optimistic excitement to the other two girls. Dottie showed Emily a list of items she had prepared to familiarize her with the DC-6, on which Emily had never flown. This flight would be credited to her training, which she would complete in Florida to become fully qualified as a DC-6 stewardess.

The three stewardesses represented a fair cross-section of American airline stewardesses: Emily Gately, who at twenty-one had flown for seven months and still thrilled with each flight; Catherine Virchow, twenty-five, poised and adept, with three and a half years' flying behind her, was ready to quit and marry; Doris Steele, thirty-four, a career stewardess with more than ten years' experience, who knew more about the airline than some men in the cockpit.

Aside from the pleasures of travel, the attraction of the stewardess' job lies in the variety of its challenges. Every day, hundreds of passengers must be handled diplomatically, some of them frightened, some ill, some boisterous and overfriendly or belligerent. In the two or three years of the average stewardess' career, a girl develops a mature poise often superior to that acquired in a finishing school or university. Responsible for supervising and serving passengers during flight, the stewardess quickly learns how to recognize, size up and cope with an infinite variety of personalities. She is trained in the rudiments of first aid and becomes adept in distinguishing true illness from the feigned. She learns to differentiate between the passenger who wants to be coddled and the one who wants to be left alone. From a man's glance or even his choice of seat, she can foretell just when he will say: "I'm going to be alone in this city . . . what do you suggest I do?" She learns how to say no, without hurting the feelings of a paying passenger, and she learns when to say yes and accept a dinner invitation. The stewardess also learns how to cope with life in a strange city between flights and she builds up a reservoir of friends of her choice along her route. It is, in short, a rewarding vocation.

The three stewardesses of Flight 823, despite the disparity in their seniority and experience, shared a staunch loyalty to Northeast Airlines. With a sense of dedication to the company's efforts to succeed in its new venture, the three girls set to work earnestly to provide their passengers with the best possible service and reasonable comfort for the flight to Miami.

Chapter Five

ONE of the early passengers aboard, Benjamin Opatowsky, a sixty-two-year-old baker from the Bronx, followed his wife Yetta to a pair of seats on the left side of the plane. Highly nervous at the prospect of flying, he spotted an emergency door on the other side and tugged at his wife, leading her to two seats near that door, by the trailing edge of the right wing. Seated near the door, he grasped the exit handle and contemplated what he would do ... just in case ...

Charles Naylor, who had worked with the Fred Waring band for nine years before becoming a free-lance pianist, composer and arranger of popular songs, led his blond wife to a double seat overlooking the left wing. Naylor, who had flown often, was solicitous: his wife was making her first airplane trip. He was explaining the advantage of sitting in the middle of the plane over a wing when he was interrupted. A stewardess requested the Naylors to move because these seats 10A and 10B had been reserved for two men who had just come aboard. The Naylors, who had booked passage through a travel agency and knew nothing about reserved seats for this flight, reluctantly gave up the wing seats to Dr. Jacob

Taub, a Bronx physician, and his brother-in-law, Dr. Benjamin Kovnat, a Manhattan dentist. The Naylors moved forward in the plane and took the first two seats in the double row. They sat there for a moment or so, facing a wooden wall at the head of the cabin, and, feeling the first symptoms of claustrophobia, decided to change seats again. They walked the length of the cabin and settled upon two seats together on the right side of the plane, three rows up from the rear lavatories. The seats there were in a triple row, and occupying the window seat was a small, frightened businessman who explained he was making his first trip in an airplane.

The Kronens, who had missed the National Airlines flight to Miami that morning, staggered aboard the plane carrying their two children, baby paraphernalia and a collapsible baby carriage. A stewardess put the carriage up forward in the buffet compartment between the cockpit and cabin, and the Kronens settled down in seats 11A and 11B, at the trailing edge of the left wing.

"Look," Ken Kronen said to his wife, "that fellow must be a basketball player." He pointed out Mason Benson, who towered above the other passengers boarding the plane. Kronen, who had played basketball for Brooklyn College, did not recognize Benson, who had been the star center of the memorable City College team of the 1940's. But Benson and his wife could hardly help being noticed. At twenty-nine, Benson still carried his 205 pounds like an athlete. Slim and broad-shouldered, he wore black slacks, black sports jacket and a bright red vest with brass buttons. His tall, slender wife, Peggy, who had once aspired to a Hollywood career, had luxuriously long red hair framing a pale face with bright green eyes.

The Bensons ensconced themselves in the last double

seat in the extreme rear on the left side of the plane. Mrs. Benson, at the window, kicked off her high-heeled shoes, rested her stockinged feet on a small piece of luggage, and opened a book. Benson idled away the time sizing up the people around him.

Norman Davis, a thirty-five-year-old mechanical engineer on a business trip, was pleased to find himself joined by a slim, attractive blonde in her early thirties. She carried three coats in addition to her hand luggage and Davis pushed his topcoat to a corner of the overhead rack and helped the young woman stow her belongings. Davis, who had had some four hundred hours' flying experience during the second World War, kept his window seat directly over the center of the left wing, the next best thing to the cockpit; like every ex-pilot, he wanted to fly the plane mentally himself. The young woman, who explained that she was a registered nurse on her way to Florida for a divorce, occupied the aisle seat.

Edward Tulowiecki, thirty-four years old and part owner of an auto and truck repair garage in South Lancaster, Massachusetts, gave the window seat 4A, just ahead of the left wing, to his excited six-year-old daughter, Nancy. This was the first vacation he had been able to afford since opening the garage with his brother after the war. No one in his family had ever flown, but after much debate, it had been decided that the most convenient and the cheapest way to get to Miami was to fly. His wife remained at home with their two younger children.

Across the aisle from the father and pigtailed daughter were Edwin Dresner, the contractor, and his wife, who vacationed in Florida every winter. The Dresners, fully equipped for Miami Beach, had checked three large suitcases and a bag of golf clubs at the ticket counter. Boarding the plane, they carried two garment bags, one packed full with dresses and the other with furs; one jewelry case, an overnight bag filled with cosmetics and two heavy cameras. Dresner took the window seat.

After the paying customers, the nonrevenue passengers came aboard. Most of the Northeast Airlines employees and their families found seats in the front of the cabin. John Reddington, the Boston ticket agent, and his wife took 1A and 1B, the first double seat on the left which had been abandoned by the Naylors. Gerry Lassell, his wife and baby chose the seats behind them. Arthur Bourgoin, the ticket agent from Augusta, and his wife settled in 1C and 1D, at the head of the column of triple seats, and Blanche Zukowski, wife of the Worcester station manager, took 2C, behind Mary Bourgoin and opposite the Lassells.

Among the last ones aboard were the Chadwicks, the mother, father and sister of the chief stewardess, who had made plans to meet that evening in a motel at the Miami Airport before going on to Miami Beach. The Chadwicks took the last seats available. Gloria was given an aisle seat behind the trailing edge of the right wing. Her mother sat two rows back and Norman Chadwick took an aisle seat in the tail section, four rows behind his daughter.

Most of the passengers soon realized that their plane was somewhat beneath the comfort standards of modern air travel. The cabin was gray and grim. It bore signs of rough wear as a cargo plane. The nineteen rows of triple seats on the right and the seventeen rows of double seats on the left were close together, leaving a minimum of leg room. The seats, which were removable, were bolted to tracks and did not line up with the windows. A passenger had to lean forward or bend back to look out a window. The upholstery was colorless and worn, the floor scuffed, and the cabin gave an over-all impression of dinginess. The raw weather did not help. The interior of the plane, unheated on the ground, was cold, and many of the women wore their coats or furs.

The Dresners had hardly settled down when Mrs. Dresner complained about the dreariness of the plane. Every seat was taken and youngsters sat on laps. Babies were crying. Mrs. Dresner did not like it at all and wanted to get off. Mr. Dresner, equally dissatisfied, knew there would be no other flight available that day. He did not want to go back home in a snowstorm, he wanted to go to Florida. "What's the matter?" he chided his wife. "This plane's not good enough for you?"

To Mrs. Chopelas, who had read many advertisements of the luxury of modern air travel, the plane seemed downright shabby. But she was not the complaining type. She leaned back in her chair, her full-length mink coat draped over her shoulders, and tried to comfort her son squirming on her lap.

To another passenger, Robert Pierce, the crowded plane looked like "a streetcar on a Saturday night." Pierce, an electrician who flew two or three times a year, watched from his window the men clearing the snow from the right wing. When the wing was cleaned, the plane still sat idle. He stopped Doris Steele as she passed. "What the hell are we sitting here now for? The snow is beginning to pile up again," he said.

"Don't worry," she replied, "everything will be all right and soon we will be down in the sunny south where there is no snow."

The trouble outside simply was the snow. It was pelting down steadily. When the men had cleaned the left wing, they moved on to the right wing and the tail surfaces; as they worked, snow piled up again on the left wing. In the cold some of the sweepers did a sort of jig while wielding their brooms and mops on the wings. This probably helped warm their feet but it did little to reassure the passengers looking out at them. Robert Pierce, the electrician, thought they were jitterbugging with brooms and mops as partners. Ed Dresner, the contractor, thought that he would not tolerate that kind of fooling by men building a house for him.

Shortly after three o'clock, the cargo and computation manifest for Flight 823 was delivered to the main door and Dottie Steele took the manifest forward to the pilot. This was another safety precaution required prior to every take-off. The pilot had to be sure that the total weight of his plane was below the maximum allowable for take-off.

Dottie Steele, commenting cheerfully that they had a fully loaded plane, handed the manifest to Captain Marsh and he ran his eyes over the figures: the plane's empty operating weight, which included the crew, came to 61,527 pounds; three thousand gallons of gasoline, 18,000 pounds; eighty-one adult passengers and six children, 13,845; cargo in the forward belly compartment, 1,160, and in the aft belly compartment, 1,290; a check stewardess, 130 pounds. The all-important figure was the total gross weight of the plane, 95,952.

At a glance Captain Marsh saw that the figure was something more than one thousand pounds below the maximum allowable take-off weight of 97,275.

Of course, he knew it would be under the allowable take-off weight. If it had been above, the load agent would have called it to the pilot's attention and some passengers would have had to get off. But the ticklish question, particularly in this marginal weather, was how closely should he approach the maximum allowable weight. The more than thousand-pound margin satisfied Captain Marsh.

Of course, no pilot can check each weight item himself. Just as he has to rely on his maintenance department for proper servicing of his plane, he has to depend on the load agent and others for the accuracy of the weights reported to him. Sitting at the controls in the cockpit, Captain Marsh had no way of knowing that there was an error of more than two thousand pounds in the weight of his plane.

The load agent, Joseph Dorrington, who prepared the weight manifest, did not suspect the error either. He relied of necessity on others for the figures which he computed.

Joe Dorrington was a new man with Northeast, but he had worked as a load agent for American Airlines for three years in Chicago. This however was a special day for him. He had made plans to fly to Miami for the weekend on Flight 823. His bag had already been loaded on the plane and he was waiting only until his relief showed up. Dorrington's duties included not only computation of the weight but the dispatch of the figures by teletype to Miami after Flight 823 left La Guardia. He had arranged with his relief, Bob Weiss, to send the message.

However, while the plane sat outside the Northeast gate, Joe Dorrington had watched the falling snow outside his window, and he changed his mind. He decided he could just as easily fly down to Miami for the weekend on Saturday morning. He cleared his change of plans with his boss, and then went on with his work.

Computation of a plane's gross weight should be a simple matter of adding up the weight of the plane and the weight of what is aboard it. That is, if everything goes right. But on some days, things do not go right.

The cargo department reported five pouches of mail at 50 pounds and seven packages of express mail at 188 pounds. The baggage checked and weighed at the airline's terminal in Manhattan and at the airport totaled 98 pieces at 2,282 pounds, but somehow, somewhere, someone made a mistake and Dorrington listed 95 bags at 2,212, thereby missing three bags at 70 pounds.

The gate agent picking up tickets from the passengers boarding through Gate 11 reported in eighty-one adults and six children, failing to pick up a ticket from one passenger in the rush to board the plane. Rather than weigh everyone boarding a plane, all adults are given a standard weight by all airlines of 160 pounds in the summer and 165 pounds in the winter. Children between two and twelve are assigned a standard weight of 80 pounds. All children under two are considered babes in arms and travel free of charge and free of weight. Dorrington, computing 165 pounds for eighty-one adults and 80 pounds for each of the six children, arrived at the total passenger weight of 13,845.

Had Dorrington checked the number of bookings, he would have found twelve adults and two children listed as through passengers from New England flights; fifty-two adults and four children booked in New York, and eighteen nonrevenue stand-by passengers, for a total of eighty-two adults and six children.

To complicate matters, at the last minute four more passengers—three adults and one child—arrived on a connecting flight from New Bedford, Massachusetts. The main cabin door of Flight 823 was reopened and the four paying passengers replaced four persons who were traveling on passes.

The stewardesses counted and recounted the passengers; no easy task, for always some passengers were moving about or using the lavatories. Finally, although no count accurately showed it, all eighty-nine seats in the cabin were occupied. There were seventy paying men and women, fourteen nonpaying, and five children. There also were six babes in arms. The plane was full, not ready to go, but full, and hardly anyone was very happy. Impatient and nervous passengers had many queries.

"When do we go?"

"How much longer will it be?"

"Is it really safe to fly in this kind of weather?"

"What're we waiting for?"

"Why is the plane so cold?"

"Are we going, or aren't we?"

The three stewardesses were busy answering questions, arranging clothing in the bulging overhead racks, taking down pillows and blankets, adjusting the reclining seats, reminding people that the NO SMOKING sign was on, warming milk for wailing babies.

Miss Steele, who had taken on most of the task of explaining the delay to complaining passengers, made a general announcement after the people had been on the plane for a half hour.

She thanked them all for their patience (although few had been anything like patient). She said the plane would depart shortly. The delay, she explained, was due partly to a mix-up in the line's new reserved-seat policy and partly to the need to clean the snow from the wings. She explained that the airplane was leased by Northeast Airlines from the Flying Tigers, the famous airline which had helped the Chinese during World War II. And she thanked them all again for their patience. Soon they would be on their way to sunny Florida.

As the senior stewardess walked down the aisle, she

explained again and again to individuals that there was nothing to worry about. Northeast Airlines had a perfect safety record. To a few passengers who wanted to leave the plane she explained that indeed they could get off, if they really wanted to, but that their luggage, stowed with that of the other passengers, would have to go on to Florida.

A passenger has, of course, every right to leave a plane and get a refund on his ticket as long as the plane is still on the ground and his leaving will not endanger the plane's safety. Passengers have been known to have done so even when the plane was on the runway preparing to take off.

But the decision is a difficult one to make. Mrs. Esther Chopelas did not want to fly in this weather. But neither did she want to disappoint her husband who would be waiting for her at Miami Airport. Mr. and Mrs. Kronen talked it over and decided it would be more troublesome getting to their home thirty minutes from the airport with the two children than to go on to Florida. Meanwhile, their children fidgeted.

In the rear of the plane, Mason Benson changed his mind about leaving the plane when his wife objected to leaving behind the jewelry that she had packed in a suitcase, now stowed away in the forward belly compartment. Diagonally across the aisle, Charles Naylor, the pianist, listened to Benson's complaints and decided that he himself would keep quiet lest he frighten his wife.

Benson idly watched the long line-up by his seat for the lavatories in the rear and smiled at the thought of so many nervous bladders. It occurred to him that if he insisted upon leaving the plane, he might well start a general exodus.

Since the first days of commercial aviation, no doubt, passengers waiting out a delay have debated inwardly whether or not to quit the plane. But it takes courage to admit one's fears to one's fellow passengers. And, if one does leave, there is always the problem of whether to return home or to board another plane and perhaps sit out another delay. One passenger on Flight 823, however, made up his mind. Dr. Taub, keeping an eye on his watch and on the falling snow, decided that if the plane did not leave by four o'clock, he would.

It was just about four o'clock when the loud-speaker clicked on and the stewardess announced that they would be leaving the ramp in a minute or two. There was a sigh of relief throughout the plane. Then she announced the plane would be taken to a hangar so that the snow could be removed from the wings properly before take-off. She again urged everyone to be patient. The temperature in Miami was 82 degrees, she said, and once they arrived there, they would forget about this delay.

The decision to take the plane inside a hangar to remove the snow was made as a last resort not to cancel the flight. When the ground crew had cleaned and sprayed the right wing with antifreeze, the left wing was completely covered with snow. John Joy sent for the maintenance supervisor, Hubert Biron. When Biron reached the plane at about 3:45, he noted a half-inch of snow on the left wing. Even half that amount would alter the air flow past the wings and endanger the plane. The shape and contour of the wings direct the flow of air over and under the wings, creating lift for the plane. Even a sixteenth of an inch of snow or ice destroys the precisely designed contour. It was equally clear that if the men swept down the left wing again, the right wing by then would become snowbound. It was a merry-go-round, the maintenance supervisor decided. Since Northeast did not have its own

hangar at La Guardia, Biron sent a mechanic, John Rohrs-
sen, to the Northeast operations office to have someone rent
facilities. The situation was explained to Captain Marsh in
the cockpit.

Operations arranged to use a nose hangar of Aircraft
Maintenance and Service Company at the extreme west end
of the field, where various companies provided repair and
maintenance services for private planes and the smaller
airlines.

The hangar was about one and a quarter miles from the
Northeast gate. Captain Marsh started up the DC-6 engines
and slowly taxied away. Biron sent a man for another drum
of Misco, the de-icing fluid, and directed the others to pile
into a truck or into the company's tug tractor to help in the
snow removal.

Inside Gate 11, several nervous relatives of passengers
abandoned their efforts to get their kin off the plane. Some,
like Joel Schwartz, left the field in the belief that the plane
was about to take off. Others, like Samuel Leider, learned
that the plane was going to a hangar and decided to wait it
out.

Inside the plane, the three stewardesses still were busy
placating passengers. "I'll probably be killed for this later,
but I'm going to serve sandwiches now," Dottie Steele told
one passenger. To another, she said with a laugh, "They'll
hand me my head when I get back, but I'm going to give
away the sandwiches we are supposed to sell later on."

The plucky stewardess felt she had enough seniority on
the line to make her own decisions. Her independence was
well known on the airline. And on this occasion, she reasoned that the best way to keep her passengers quiet and
happy was to feed them. As the plane taxied slowly through
the snow, both Kay Virchow and Emily Gately set up

trays at the buffet with assorted sandwiches, small salads, cake and coffee.

There was no question of letting passengers out of the plane while it was being cleaned. It was essential that they stay aboard so that once the plane was ready, it could take off before accumulating too much more snow or ice.

Taxiing slowly to the hangar, Captain Marsh switched on the heat for the wings and tail section. Glancing out his side window, he could see snow blowing off his left wing. It did not seem as though he would have much of a problem with ice or snow once the plane was cleaned and coated with antifreeze in the hangar.

Moving slowly and cautiously, it took some twenty-five minutes to reach the hangar. There a hangar tractor was hooked up and the plane was pushed carefully inside. The Northeast men arrived with their own tractor in time to help complete the job. The big plane was pushed all the way in so that its white nose was only a foot from the inside wall.

The hangar, however, was what is commonly called a nose hangar. It was a kind of shed having a back wall and two side walls, and an open front end with canvas curtains. It accommodated only two-thirds of the plane. When the curtains were drawn, the hangar enclosed the plane only to the trailing edge of the wings. The aft part of the fuselage and the big tail section remained outside in the snow.

Once the plane was in place, its wheels chocked with blocks, the mechanics and cleaners attacked the snow again. They pushed ladders and platform stands up to the wings inside the hangar and to the horizontal stabilizers on the tail outside the hangar. Another full drum of antifreeze was mixed into the high-pressure spray rig to the proportion of 75 per cent Misco and 25 per cent water. After an area was swept clean—and the snow came off easily—it was sprayed with Misco, which left an even coating of fluid, thicker than but not unlike automobile antifreeze.

A stairway was moved up to the crew door in the cockpit, and Captain Marsh, Dixwell and Andon left the plane to stretch their legs and drink some hot coffee in the hangar's office.

The passengers were kept inside, where Dottie Steele distributed dinner trays. Because the center aisle barely allowed the stewardesses to pass one another, Kay Virchow and Emily Gately confined their work to the buffet area where they set up trays for the senior stewardess. Serving some ninety-five people presented a problem in logistics. By the time the energetic Miss Steele worked her way to the passengers in the rear, those up front were demanding more coffee, or more food, or both.

Dottie Steele was kept as busy cajoling passengers to remain aboard as she was serving food. Once she passed on to Walter Peto, the Northeast station manager, a passenger's request to deplane, but he gave the reply she expected: Yes, a passenger could get off the plane, but could not reclaim luggage.

The only passengers who did not complain were Northeast employees. They were happy that they had not been bumped. In the first two rows of seats, Blanche Zukowski met the Lassells across the aisle and they in turn met the Reddingtons. Arthur Bourgoin passed his time talking with his wife and reassuring a woman in the window seat that the safety of the plane was assured by the multitude of government regulations covering bad-weather flying.

In the rear of the plane, Charles Naylor, the pianist, tried to sleep but could not because of repeated queries, complaints and demands. The tall, handsome man in the rear, in particular, made his demands known to the stewardess and to anyone else in earshot.

Mason Benson had not been appeased when Dottie Steele told him she had saved her own de luxe roast beef sandwich for him and his wife. The de luxe sandwich was a thin slice of beef, well done, between slices of dry bread. As he pointed out to his wife, they had not minded going by the coach flight because it was scheduled to arrive in Miami at about seven o'clock; but it was now past five, and since they would arrive too late to enjoy the evening there, they could just as well go the next day.

"I'd like to speak to the captain, if you don't mind," he told the stewardess, after losing a lengthy argument with her about getting off the plane.

"You can't," she said.

"Why not?" he demanded.

"Because he's not here. He left the plane," she said, "and besides, we have no stairway to let passengers off at this hangar."

"Well," said Benson, "if he got off, I would like to get off also—through the nose, if possible."

"If you insist, of course, you can get off, but there is no transportation to the terminal. You'll be stuck here a couple of hours, at least, and it won't be long now—a few minutes —before we get going."

Mrs. Benson, somewhat embarrassed by the debate, nudged her husband. "As long as it'll be a couple of minutes more, let's stick it out . . . we waited this long."

Benson desisted. It was only a matter of minutes before Dottie Steele edged her way back to him and said the captain was back on the plane and that they would soon be on their way. Benson waited and once again read the printed directions for opening the emergency window beside his seat.

A few minutes before 5:30, Captain Marsh and his crew, informed that the plane was ready to go, climbed the ramp back toward the cockpit. They paused at the top step of the ramp and looked over the plane. It seemed clean, except for a few patches of snow along the top of the fuselage. But even that snow was dripping off in the warmth of the hangar.

The crew climbed aboard without any closer inspection of the plane. But Joy, the lead mechanic, had worked on the tail section himself and had made sure that the trim tab, the hinges and the other moving parts of the tail, which had been exposed to the elements during the cleaning, were clear of snow and ice. No one, however, bothered to test the reaction of rudder and ailerons to the cockpit controls.

A tow bar was attached and the tractor pulled the plane slowly out of the nose hangar. The plane was a good way out before the tug lost traction in the snow. The ground crew and Marsh conferred and agreed to try reverse thrust of the engines. Moving a plane in reverse on the ground heavily taxes and overheats the engines, but a few seconds' reverse thrust would not normally hurt a plane. Marsh started up all four engines. The lights dimmed inside the cabin and passengers found something new to worry about.

"Watch the temperatures," Captain Marsh told his flight engineer. He moved the throttles to reverse and released his brakes. The big plane roared and shuddered. Passengers fidgeted uncomfortably in their seats. The plane skidded to the right as its tail swung to the left. Within seconds, Marsh cut the engines, before the plane could hit anything.

Fire flared in the exhaust pipe of No. 2, the left inboard engine, but it was quickly doused with a carbon dioxide extinguisher by mechanic Pete Tsante, who was standing fire guard. Stack fires, which occur when a spark ignites excess gasoline in an engine exhaust pipe, are fairly common in starting up large aircraft and are not in the least dangerous. This stack fire was handled so routinely that the crew in the cockpit was not even aware of it.

The problem was not the fire, but how to get the plane out of the hangar. The hangar tractor pushed the Northeast tractor in an effort to get better traction and to swing the airplane away from the hangar, but this also failed. Then Captain Marsh suggested that he could use forward thrust on No. 1, the left outboard engine, while the tugs pulled on the right side of the plane to swing it clear of the hangar.

Again the plane roared, and this time its wheels, which had been blocked by the snow, jumped clear and the lumbering plane swung free of the hangar.

Getting out of the hangar had taken close to fifteen minutes. It had proved bothersome to the ground and cockpit crew, and had further frayed the nerves of those aboard the plane. But now, finally, three hours past their scheduled departure, they were ready to go.

Chapter Six

LARGE wet snowflakes fell steadily from the darkling sky as Flight 823 cleared the nose hangar. To the layman, it was a heavy snowfall. But for flying purposes, the U. S. Weather Bureau measures snowfall in terms of visibility obscured. Thus it was "light snow" to the airport weather bureau. Visibility had ranged between one-half and one mile most of the day, and it made no difference that 5.8 inches of snow had shrouded metropolitan New York, snarling all surface transportation.

Standing in this "light snow," one of the ground crew signaled the cockpit: "All clear to start." The signal released the plane from the maintenance department and informed the pilot that the area around the plane which he could not see from the cockpit was clear of anyone who might be hurt by the revving of the propellers.

It was almost 5:45. This would be a night flight for Alva Marsh and his crew, who had gone on duty that day at about 7:30 in the morning.

The three men in the cockpit again began the ritual of starting up the four engines. If anyone still cherishes the image of a pilot, in white scarf and goggles, jumping into a bucket seat in the cockpit, pushing a button or two and flying off into the wild blue yonder, he need only witness the complex procedures governing today's transport planes.

Before switching on the ignition, Flight Engineer Andon read off nineteen items on the *pre-start* check list, each item requiring a response from the captain, first officer or himself: "Battery and external power . . . inverters . . . parking brake . . . hydraulic and air brake pressure . . . hydraulic fluid . . . heaters . . . fuel, oil and ADI quantity . . . cabin pressure . . . landing gear down . . . crew oxygen . . . navigation lights . . . flight instruments . . ." And the responses as one man or another checked each control, gauge or dial: "On . . . checked . . . set . . ."

Finally Captain Marsh gave the order to start engines in the usual order, 3, 4, 2, 1. Andon opened the engine cowl flaps to allow a maximum of air to circulate around the engines while the plane taxied on the ground. Captain Marsh advanced the four throttles to one-quarter of full power. Andon set the fuel-boost pump on low, dialed the engine selector to No. 3 and reached for the starter switch in the center overhead panel. With his middle finger on the starter switch and his thumb on a safety switch below, he squeezed. This rotated No. 3 propeller which distributed throughout that engine any oil or fuel accumulated in the bottom cylinders. When the three-bladed propeller had revolved twice, Dixwell called out, "Six blades." Captain Marsh ordered, "Start." Andon flicked on the ignition switch and, at the same time, pushed his index finger down on the ignition boost switch and his third finger down on the primer switch, which fed raw gasoline into the engine. The engine fired, and Captain Marsh watched the r.p.m. rise to between 600 and 800 and then he brought up the fuel mixture control handle to auto-rich. Andon waited until he heard the engine running smoothly, then released both the prime and boost switches to allow the engine to run on its own power. Thus was No. 3 engine started. The men then repeated the procedure to start Engines 4, 2 and 1.

When all four engines were running smoothly, Captain Marsh ascertained that he had the plane's weight manifest aboard, Engineer Andon checked the fire warning system, and the door warning lights, which indicated that all exterior doors were closed and secured. Then Marsh signaled to the ground crew that he was ready to go. Through his side window, he saluted the man on the ground. From here on, he legally assumed all responsibility for the plane and the flight. A return salute from the ground man was the captain's receipt. Flying time and pay would be computed from now until he shut down the engines at his destination. The ground man clocked the time at 5:45 P.M.

But before moving the plane, the men in the cockpit went over nine more items on the check list for taxiing. Andon lowered the wing flaps to the maximum 50 degrees and raised them back to zero to check their freedom of movement. Then he set them at 20 degrees down, which gave the wings a convexity that added lift for the take-off; the more lift the wings provided, the shorter the take-off run.

Andon also checked the carburetor heat and the electrical output of the generators. Then he switched on the pump for ADI (antidetonation injection) fluid for a wet take-off. The injection of water into the engines on take-off, a common practice in transport planes, cools the interior of the engines while they are under the tremendous strain of lifting the aircraft off the ground. The cooling water, which is then spewed out the exhaust, allows an engine to develop approximately three hundred additional horsepower.

Marsh and Dixwell then determined the proper take-off speeds for the plane's gross weight. The men were concerned with two speeds, which must be computed for the take-off of every airliner. One—the V_1 speed—is the maximum at which the plane can be braked to a safe stop on the runway in the event of an emergency. The other—V_2—is the speed at which the plane should be lifted off the runway.

These essential speeds are calculated in the operations manual for the plane according to gross weight and other factors, against the possibility of engine failure at the most critical point in the take-off. Every airliner is designed to be flown safely at these speeds even if the most critical engine—usually the left outboard engine—fails on take-off.

For this flight, Marsh and Dixwell figured V_1 speed at 90 knots and take-off V_2 speed at 110.

With all preparations accomplished, Captain Marsh taxied the plane slowly through the snow away from the hangar area to clear the buildings which might impede radio communication with the control tower.

Radio communication in the cockpit is the primary responsibility of the co-pilot. Dixwell got the latest weather report for La Guardia Airport: "Precipitation ceiling 500 [feet], sky obscured; visibility ¾ [mile] with light snow and fog; wind: north northeast 12 [knots]."

This was well above the airport's approved minimums for four-engine take-offs: 200-foot ceiling and one-quarter-mile visibility. But it was marginal weather.

Alva Marsh could have canceled the flight at this point—or at any point up to take-off. He needed only to report snow accumulating on his wings, or he could simply have

89]

voiced his own judgment that weather conditions were not suitable for flying. The company would have been disappointed at the loss of revenue and the upset of the schedule, but it would have had to accept the pilot's decision. Marsh's wife, Ann, would have been disappointed, but pilots' wives grow accustomed to weather-bound husbands away from home. Al Marsh himself would have been put out at having to stay overnight in New York. And his passengers would have grumbled over a trip aborted after three hours of waiting.

There were also the immeasurable factors, which are present in almost all of the decisions of whether or not to fly in marginal weather. Even Captain Marsh himself could not know whether he would have taken off that night, under the same conditions, had he lived in New York and been leaving his family rather than returning to it. Then there is the matter of prestige and reputation. A pilot who cancels too often in bad weather may become known as a "fair-weather flier." The professional pilot is paid well for being able to cope with the elements. In fact, many commercial pilots welcome bad weather as a test of their ability and as a relief from the monotony of fair-weather flying. Such were some of the immeasurable aspects in Captain Marsh's problem of whether or not to fly that night.

Taxiing out to the runway, Alva Marsh decided to postpone his final decision until the last minute before take-off. The one decisive factor would be whether or not there was snow on his wings at the start of his take-off roll. So, he asked his co-pilot to check into the control tower for clearance to the runway.

"La Guardia Ground Control, Northeast Flight Eight-Twenty-Three, taxiing out from Butler, IFR Miami," said Dixwell, reporting the plane in the Butler service area on the southwestern side of the field and asking for clearance for their instrument-flight route to Miami.

Nine men handled the traffic at La Guardia Field from a glass-enclosed oval room, about 11½ by 22 feet, atop the control tower. On an eight-hour shift, the men rotated positions every two hours so that none might crack under the strain.

Dixwell's message was only one in a flurry of conversations being carried on with the Airport Ground Controller. Joseph Maye, the controller handling ground traffic, was particularly busy because of many requests from plane crews for clearance to taxi to hangars for de-icing before take-off. No plane could move on the ground without his permission.

"Is that Northeast Eight-Twenty-Three?" he asked, just to be sure.

"That's affirmative," said Dixwell.

"You say you're leaving Butler?"

"Ah, we just came across the road."

The controller, noting the flight number and destination on an eight-by-five-inch sheet of white paper, cleared the flight to the run-up position:

"Northeast Eight-Twenty-Three, cleared to Runway Four. The wind is northeast one-zero. Proceed via Taxiway Two. Hold short of Runway Four. Over."

Joe Maye flicked his talk-listen switch to hear the flight repeat his instructions. "Okay, uh, to Taxiway Two, will hold short of, uh, Runway Four," came the voice from Flight 823.

"That's correct, Northeast Eight-Twenty-Three. The altimeter, three-zero-one-two. The time, one-fi . . . correction . . . one seven four seven and one-half."

In the plane, Marsh and Dixwell checked their panel clocks to read 5:47½ P.M. and calibrated their altimeters to the correct barometric pressure.

While Marsh moved the plane slowly down the taxiway, Andon went back into the main cabin to make sure that the main door was securely locked. Some passengers were surprised to see an officer from the cockpit in the cabin while the plane was moving. Andon was complying with a regulation that required the flight engineer or first officer of every pressurized passenger plane to check the main cabin door visually; the door warning lights in the cockpit are not considered sufficient. The regulations grew out of an incident aboard an airliner in July, 1952, when the main cabin door, which had not been securely closed, flew open at 12,000 feet near Rio de Janeiro and a woman passenger was sucked out of the plane to her death.

Through small inspection portholes Andon could see the locking mechanism levers inside the main cabin door. The levers and locks were painted a bright color so that, when properly locked, the engineer could spot at a glance a straight line between the levers and the locks. Any break in the line would indicate a lever was not properly in place. The engineer also checked the evacuation slide attached to the main door which, in the event of emergency, could be sprung like a parachute by a stewardess.

When Andon returned to the cockpit, the three stewardesses were still scurrying up and down the narrow center aisle to pick up the remaining dinner trays.

The FASTEN SEAT BELTS sign flashed on in the front of the cabin. Gerry Lassell, the instrument mechanic, wrapped the loose end of his belt around the secured part and knotted it. But when his wife, Marilyn, tried to wrap the belt around Roy, their eighteen-month-old son, Lassell said,

"No, we don't want it that way. Put it around yourself and hold on to him." A former Air Force man, he personally checked the belts before he relaxed.

While picking up trays, the stewardesses tried to observe that each passenger had the seat belt on correctly. It was no easy task in a crowded plane, and the girls overlooked Mrs. Chopelas in a middle seat. She was afraid she would not be able to get out of the plane in the event of a crash if she were strapped into her seat. So she put her two-year-old son, Gregory, squarely on her lap, wrapped her mink coat around herself and the boy, and left the belt unbuckled.

At the trailing edge of the left wing, Kenneth Kronen, ever fascinated by the absurdity that planes could fly, was looking out his window at the wing. "What was the use of going into the hangar anyway?" he asked his wife. "The wings are as full of snow as before we went in. . . ."

In the seat ahead, Dr. Taub complained to his brother-in-law. "What a ridiculous situation this is. The plane is all covered with snow again and they've decided to take off. . . ."

Two seats farther up, Norman Davis, who had been through pilot training in the second World War, reasoned that the pilot had to know what he was doing and that if the plane was taking off, the weather was all right.

The door to the buffet and beyond that the top half of a Dutch door leading to the cockpit were open. Davis could see the three men at work in the cockpit, which was illuminated by a dim white bulb. They were checking their instruments as the plane taxied to the head of the runway, and Dixwell was getting clearance.

When Dixwell had first asked for clearance for Flight 823 at 5:47 P.M., Ground Controller Maye had handed the request, which he had jotted on the eight-by-five-inch sheet of paper, to Fred Prawdzik, the flight data processor, who sat next to him.

While Maye directed the plane's taxiing to the head of the runway, Prawdzik passed the clearance request via direct telephone to the Air Route Traffic Control Center at Idlewild Airport.

"Clearance Northeast eight-two-three."

In a 40-by-220-foot room, the nerve center of about four million dollars' worth of airport radar equipment, a route man checked Flight 823's proposed instrument-flight plan against other flights in the New York area and en route. The plan, which had been filed earlier that afternoon, had been held in abeyance until the flight was ready to go. Once it had been checked, the route man gave his clearance and the pilot's first check point.

"Belle Mead seven thousand."

In the La Guardia tower, Prawdzik time-stamped the clearance sheet and gave it to Maye. In the verbal shorthand used in control towers, Ground Controller Maye passed the word to the plane.

"Northeast Eight-Twenty-Three, cleared to Belle Mead. Maintain seven-thousand." Northeast acknowledged by repeating the instructions. Then Maye continued: "After take-off, a left turn direct Paterson; direct Chatham, cross the zero-eight-one degree radial of Caldwell [at] four thousand or above; cross Paterson between five and six thousand and cross the northwest course of Idlewild not above six thousand."

Dixwell rapidly repeated the instructions back to the tower. Maye, without breaking stride, turned to his next problem, an Eastern Airlines twin-engine plane reporting in. "La Guardia Ground Control, Eastern Five-Eighty-

Seven, we're down here at the hangar and we're ready to taxi out for take-off."

Maye gave him clearance to Runway 4, and told him the wind velocity was ten knots, from the northeast. "Hold short of United [Airlines] area," Maye ordered. "Have a United DC-6 taxiing into his area proceeding eastbound on the ramp. . . ." Then, to an airliner which had just landed, he said, "United Six-Forty-Four, cleared to gate. . . ."

Maye, now handling three planes at once, turned back to Northeast Flight 823: "Uh, Northeast Two-Eighty-. . . correction, Eight-Twenty-Three, your position now?"

"Eight-Twenty-Three is ready to cross the runway," answered Dixwell. No pilot on a busy airport would think of crossing an active runway without permission from the tower.

"Eight-Twenty-Three, stand by," said Maye. Then, a moment later, after checking the traffic, Maye waved Flight 823 on. "Eight-Twenty-Three, cleared to cross Runway Four. Best time. Advise when clear." Maye then cleared the incoming United flight to his unloading gate and instructed the departing Eastern flight to taxi to the run-up position for take-off from Runway 4.

Captain Marsh maneuvered carefully through the snow across the runway on to the run-up position, a semicircular parking area at the extreme end of the 4,963-foot runway. He held his aircraft at about a 90-degree angle to the runway, checking that his C-2 gyrosyn compass read 280 degrees, which was almost due west.

Then, Andon brought out the check list and called off the items for revving up the engines, first the outboard engines 1 and 4 together, then the inboard engines 2 and 3. He looked quickly but methodically at each of the twenty-four gauges on his powerplant instrument board for the correct oil and fuel pressures and the correct temperatures on the engine cylinder heads.

As the plane throbbed with power, Dottie Steele called out to the other two stewardesses, "Well, I guess this is it." Emily Gately closed the bottom half of the Dutch door between the buffet area and the cabin and made her way gingerly down the length of the plane to her small wall seat in the extreme rear. Dottie Steele went through the cabin, telling passengers who still had their dinner trays to put them under their seats. Kay Virchow tried to return a few more trays to the buffet before take-off. It was against regulations to have loose trays about on take-off, but it also was against regulations—and far more dangerous —to have anyone standing or moving around. Dottie and Kay made for their seats, which faced the rear of the plane, just in front of the main cabin door. They quickly fastened their belts. Passengers braced themselves for the take-off.

In the cockpit, Dixwell reported to the tower: "Northeast Eight-Twenty-Three is clear."

"Northeast Eight-Twenty-Three 'is clear,' thank you," repeated the ground controller in the tower. "And your type of equipment?"

"A DC-6," replied Dixwell.

"Thank you," said Maye, noting down the information and handing the sheet of paper concerning Flight 823 to the local controller, Herbert Goodman, who directed take-off and landing traffic at the airport. His was the busiest and most critical post in the tower, but Goodman, with ten years' service, was the most experienced man in the room. He also was supervisor of the 4–12 P.M. watch.

Meanwhile, Dixwell, changing his radio frequency for take-off instructions, listened in on Goodman clearing the landings of a United Airlines flight followed by a private plane. Then the Eastern Airlines plane, bound for Washington, D.C., which had followed Marsh's DC-6 to the run-up position, asked for take-off clearance.

"Eastern Five-Eight-Seven, we have traffic on short final. Advise when he lands, please," said Goodman.

"Okay," replied M. G. Cummings, Jr., co-pilot of the Eastern plane. "It looks like we got a Northeast airplane sitting up here in front of us, though."

Dixwell, taking this opportunity to break into the rapid-fire radio talk, reported in to the local controller: "Uh, Tower, Northeast Eight-Twenty-Three."

"Northeast Eight-Twenty-Three, stand by," said Goodman.

The controller brought in the two planes, cleared them off the main runway, then said: "Okay, Northeast Eight-Twenty-Three, no delay, clear take-off Runway Four. Traffic at the outer marker."

Thus at 5:55 P.M. Northeast Flight 823 was cleared for take-off with instructions to tune its radio to the radar departure controller when past the airport's outer boundary.

"Okay, Eight-Twenty-Three, we're getting into position," reported Dixwell, as Marsh swung the plane around and, steering by the nose wheel, moved the aircraft slowly toward the runway. The snow was firmly packed by previous traffic and steering was difficult, as the plane tended to slide. "It's slippery out here," Dixwell commented to the tower because of the extra time it took them to get the plane into position.

From the tower it was impossible to see any aircraft at the start of the runway. Three huge American Airlines hangars to the left of the tower obscured the first 1,000 to 2,000 feet of the runway. Controller Goodman was busy, mentally juggling the impending take-offs of Northeast and Eastern planes and the imminent landing of an American Airlines DC-6.

"Eastern Five-Eighty-Seven," Goodman called, "move up close to but remain clear of Runway Four, please."

"Okay, Eastern Five-Eighty-Seven," came the answer.

The controller, wondering if the Northeast flight had begun its take-off but not wanting to distract the Northeast pilot at the critical moment, asked the crew of the Eastern plane at the edge of the runway, "Eastern Five-Eighty-Seven, has that aircraft started its roll yet?"

"Negative."

"Northeast Eight-Twenty-Three," called the controller, "clear the runway. The traffic's in close now. It took you too long to get into position."

Marsh swung the plane off the runway as Dixwell told the tower, "Okay, Eight-Twenty-Three, we're clearing."

"Okay, sir," said the tower. "Let me know as soon as you clear, Eight-Twenty-Three."

A moment later, Dixwell announced the plane was clear of the runway, and Goodman told the arriving American Airlines flight to come in. "American One-Sixty-Eight, clear to land Runway Four."

At almost the same time, a privately owned plane announced to the tower it was holding at Flatbush, waiting for clearance to make its approach.

"Thirty-Alpha," Goodman called back, "you're number two for Runway Four. Traffic short final. The wind is north northeast ten [knots]."

The messages flashed back and forth and the two planes put down on the runway, speeding by the waiting Northeast and Eastern planes. Then Goodman cleared Marsh again to the head of the runway. "Okay, Eight-Twenty-

Three, I think he [the private plane landing] just touched down. Taxi right into position on Runway Four and hold."

"Eight-Twenty-Three, he's by. We're moving," announced Dixwell, and Captain Marsh moved the plane to the head of the runway. There, the men went through the final check list again before the actual take-off. Gust locks, which kept the ailerons, rudder and elevators from flapping in the wind when the plane was on the ground, now were released. The gust lock handle was down and latched. Captain Marsh checked the full travel of all his flight controls. He swung the control wheel in front of him to the left and right to test the ailerons, pushed it forward and eased it back to move the elevators. He depressed the right and left rudder pedals to fan the rudder. Andon set the engine cowls at four degrees for the proper cooling of the engines on take-off.

Then, with everything done that the book required, they waited for word from the tower. "Northeast Eight-Twenty-Three, cleared for take-off, Runway Four," came the clearance, and Marsh kicked off the brakes. With his right hand covering the four throttle handles on the center pedestal, he advanced the throttles slowly and firmly to the maximum power setting. The engines responded in crescendo and the big white plane began to move down the runway.

In seconds it would reach V_1 speed, the point of no return. It was Captain Marsh's last chance to decide on flying or canceling. Still concerned about the weather but realizing the importance of the flight to Northeast, Marsh decided to base his decision on whether or not the snow was being blown off his wings during the first stage of his take-off roll.

He still could have aborted this flight in good conscience. Others had during that afternoon and evening: American Airlines canceled forty-five departures, Eastern eight, and Capital six flights out of La Guardia. Since 2:45 P.M., when Al Marsh had been scheduled to depart, only twenty-seven planes had taken off. But Marsh could not know this at the time.

As Marsh pushed the throttles forward, Flight Engineer Andon followed the movement with his own right hand on the duplicate set of throttles on the left side of the control pedestal. Dixwell used both hands to press forward on the control wheel to keep the nose of the plane down and get better traction in the snow. Marsh devoted his primary attention to maneuvering the plane by the nose steering wheel located to the left of his lap. At the start of the roll, the plane skidded from side to side on the slick snow-covered runway.

But as the speed picked up to between forty and fifty knots, Marsh—with two or three maneuvers of the rudder —brought the plane smartly to the center of the 150-foot-wide runway. At the same time, he reached over his head and flicked on his wing inspection lights. He looked out to ascertain that the cowl flaps were closing on the engines. Open cowl flaps, as small as they are, can seriously compromise the performance of the plane on a critical take-off.

Then, bending at the waist, Marsh leaned as far to his left as he could to observe the left wing. Dixwell observed the right wing. Through the cockpit's small side windows they could see only part of the wings, from about the engines to the outer tips of the wings along the leading edges. They could not see the area inboard of the engines or the trailing edges of the wings. The wings were white with snow, but it appeared to them that the blast of the propellers was blowing the stuff off the wings, and the Misco applied in the hangar seemed to be keeping the snow from sticking.

Al Marsh was satisfied.

"Give me take-off power," he told his flight engineer.

Andon adjusted the throttles individually for synchronization so that each tachometer read 2,800 r.p.m. and the manifold pressure leveled off at $59\frac{1}{2}$ inches on each engine. Captain Marsh kept one hand loosely on the throttles so that he still could stop in the event of an emergency before reaching V_1 speed.

With his eyes on the speed indicator, Dixwell called out, "Ninety-six knots." That was the V_1 speed: they were committed to take off.

Now, Dixwell took his hands from the control wheel. Getting the plane off the ground was solely up to Marsh. This is a captain's moment of greatest tension: his life depends on getting the plane airborne and there is no turning back. Altitude provides his only safety.

With all his years of flying, Al Marsh was comparatively new to the DC-6. This plane was much different from the twin-engine Convairs he had been flying: it was larger, heavier, and it had twice as many engines and almost double the number of instruments. His experience in it added up to only eighty-odd hours.

As the plane, roaring down the runway, built up still more speed, the two pilots saw the snow-covered ground slip away beneath them. The speed indicator needle moved up, and Dixwell announced, "One hundred ten." That was V_2.

Marsh eased back on the control wheel, first taking up the slack and then applying pressure to draw the wheel back toward his body. The nose of the plane responded by rising into the air.

In the La Guardia tower, Controller Goodman could not see the start of the take-off roll so he asked the Eastern Airlines plane, waiting at the head of the runway, "Eastern Five-Eighty-Seven, will you advise when that DC-6 starts his roll?"

"He's already going," came the reply, and at that instant, Goodman saw the lights of the plane illuminating the runway ahead of the nearest American Airlines hangar. Then he saw the DC-6, with the familiar beacon of its Grimes light revolving atop its fuselage, itself speeding down the runway.

The take-off of Flight 823 appeared normal to Captain Bost in the Eastern plane on the ground and to Controller Goodman in the tower. The DC-6 seemed to break ground somewhere between halfway and two-thirds of the way down the runway.

Goodman observed the wheels leave the ground and noted the time of take-off: 6:01 P.M. Then he handed the dispatch sheet to the departure control man at the radar set, who would monitor the flight to its first check point.

Goodman then called Flight 823 with his last instructions: "Northeast Eight-Twenty-Three, contact departure [control] One-Two-Zero-Point-Four [radio frequency]."

"Eight-Twenty-Three," Dixwell acknowledged. That was the last message from Flight 823.

In the cabin, the passengers, oblivious to the intricacies of a take-off, were experiencing a mixture of trepidation and relief.

To the worried Dr. Taub, everything seemed awry. The snow was frightening, the night black and the engines none too powerful. "Ben," he said to his brother-in-law in the window seat over the left wing, "pray for a long runway. Look down and tell me if those wheels are leaving the ground."

To Kenneth Kronen, seated behind Dr. Taub but at the window, the engines seemed to roar with an abundance of power which thrilled him. Holding his infant son in his arms, the young salesman watched as the white runway lights, two hundred feet apart, sped by his window, and his excitement rose with the plane.

In the tail section, the beautiful Mrs. Benson still was buried in her book. Her husband, looking out the window, glimpsed a large white sign at the end of the runway, and jokingly said: "If you can read that sign, honey, you're as good as dead."

"What did it say?" she asked.

"That's exactly what it said: 'If you can read this sign, you are as good as dead,' " Benson said with a smile.

Joan Sanger, a young Scarsdale housewife, tightened her grip on her arm rests as the plane surged forward. At her side, her three-year-old daughter, Mindy, unconcernedly munched the remains of a sandwich.

Across the aisle and up a ways, six-year-old Nancy Tulowiecki was filling in the pictures in her coloring book.

Arthur Bourgoin had been perfectly calm when he had boarded the plane, but with the three-hour delay his composure ebbed away. As the plane began to move down the runway, he noted the location of the emergency door near his seat and read the instructions for opening it. At his side, his wife, Mary, crossed her fingers. Behind her, Mrs. Zukowski closed her eyes and, as always when she took off or landed in a plane, began intoning the Lord's Prayer: "Our Father, who art in Heaven . . ."

Across the aisle, in seat 1-A, John Reddington nudged his wife, leaned back and closed his eyes, and said, "Wake me when we reach Miami."

Chapter Seven

WHEN the plane left the ground, Captain Marsh did two things. He ordered "Gear up!" and he began to fly the DC-6 by instruments alone.

Andon reached forward to the pedestal between the two pilots. He squeezed the gear handle and then pulled it straight up, hydraulically lifting the two belly wheels and the nose wheel into the fuselage. A small red light flashed on to indicate the landing gear was in transit. It took the three wheels twelve seconds to retract fully into the fuselage, giving the plane clean lines for flight.

The three men heard the gear lock in place with a click which broke the silence of the cockpit. The red light went out. Conversation in a cockpit on any take-off is strictly limited to operations. Peripheral talk can divert a man's attention or lead to a dangerous misunderstanding. (An Air Force pilot broke the rule once, during a routine take-off, to exhort his co-pilot, who was having family trouble, to "Cheer up." The co-pilot pulled the *gear up*. The plane, still rolling down the runway, did not get off the ground again for a long time.)

First Officer Dixwell, glancing at the tachometer, noted that No. 1 engine was over-revving to 2,900 r.p.m. He leaned over and tog-gled back a little switch which brought the engine down to 2,800 r.p.m. in synchronization with the other three. At the same time, Andon toggled another switch to bring down the BMEP on No. 1 to 240. (BMEP is aviation short-hand for brake mean effective pressure, which in English is the engine's horsepower output. The 240 is shorthand for 2,400 horsepower.) The manifold pressures, another index of engine performance, remained even at 59½ inches on all four engines.

As soon as the plane was airborne, Captain Marsh turned his entire attention to his flight instrument panel where eleven dials and gauges were shock-mounted in three rows to tell him how high his plane was, how fast it was going, whether it was climbing, level or descending and in which direction it was going. For safety's sake there were not one but two or three instruments that cross-checked one an-other.

In a small plane, a pilot can fly by the seat of his pants: if he sits lightly, he knows he is descending; if he sits heav-ily, he is climbing. He can listen with an experienced ear to the sound of his single engine and use his eyes to guide him in flight.

But an airliner pilot flies by the gauges. In a heavy, multi-engine plane, his senses are not enough; in fact, they may lure him into dangerous illusions. So, even in clear and sunny weather, he must go on instruments, as Marsh did, as soon as the plane is airborne. The transition from visual to instrument flying must be fast: it is critical.

Once on instruments, the pilot must not look away from them. The instruments tell him what the plane is doing, and to look away is not to know. Blindfolded, a bird will crash to the ground in sensory confusion, and a pilot who looks away from his instruments, when instrument flying is necessary, is a blindfolded bird.

The professional pilot "reads" his instruments as other people read a book, not word by word but phrase by phrase or sentence by sentence for the over-all meaning. No one instrument tells the pilot all he needs to know about his flight. Each instrument refers to another and the pilot interprets the points of information into a language which tells him, without looking out the window, what his plane is doing. In reading his panel board, the average pilot observes 120 instruments per minute, or two instruments every second. Cameras hidden behind instrument panels to study pilots' eye movements in test flights have shown that the eyes pause only when something is amiss.

Captain Marsh was reading his entire instrument panel, but he was concentrating on three essential factors for this take-off: airspeed, rate of climb and direction.

Flight 823 had not yet passed the dike at the end of Runway 4 when Captain Marsh made his first scan of the instrument panel. He noted that the rate-of-climb indicator —a needle and dial that resembled a one-handed clock pointing to 9—showed the plane was climbing at 800 feet a minute. The altimeter had started upward, although it was too soon for a precise reading. The turn-and-bank needle and ball were wavering but indicated a normal configuration, and the artificial horizon showed the plane in a normal nose-up position. The C-2 gyrosyn compass needle was oscillating normally between forty and forty-five degrees.

Because of past pilot squawks about the gyrosyn compass in the plane, Captain Marsh was depending more on his automatic radio direction finder than the compass for the heading of the plane. The ADF gauge in the second row of his instrument panel was in fact two radio direction finders. The No. 2 ADF, indicated by a double needle in the dial, was set to point to the La Guardia Field transmitter located at Clasons Point in the Bronx, 2.8 miles directly ahead of Runway 4. By following this heading needle, Captain Marsh could ascertain that he was flying in a straight line from the runway. The No. 1 ADF, indicated by a single needle in the same dial, had been set to the Paterson, New Jersey, radio range station so that once Marsh passed Clasons Point, he could turn left to align the plane with the No. 1 ADF needle and head for Paterson.

The La Guardia and Paterson transmitters emitted low-frequency radio signals which are influenced by electricity in the air, particularly in storms. These stations had long since been augmented and sometimes replaced by expensive very high-frequency (VHF) installations that, like FM radio, were unaffected by static. Captain Marsh had two VHF navigational systems in the cockpit but as an old-timer he preferred not to use the new system early in the flight.

Captain Marsh had still another navigational radio, his instrument-landing system, which had been tuned to the glide path back into Runway 4 so that in an emergency he could swing his plane around for an instrument approach back to Runway 4.

Despite the heavy snowfall and fog, there was relatively little air turbulence. The plane handled smoothly. Captain Marsh had only to move his control wheel and rudder pedals slightly to correct for minor deviations from course as the plane climbed away from the ground. His movements were instinctive, like those of an expert motorist keeping his car on the highway.

First Officer Dixwell read his own instrument panel, double-checking the captain on the crucial period of the flight. His eyes scanned his altimeter, rate-of-climb and airspeed indicators, his compass, ADF, turn-and-bank needle and artificial horizon. Neither man looked out the window: their eyes were glued to their instruments.

When the speed indicator needle reached 125 knots, Captain Marsh called out, "Zero flaps." Dixwell, observing the same reading, reached forward and moved the flap handle to the neutral position. He glanced at the flap indicator in the center of the power instrument panel; it told him the flaps were moving from 20 degrees to zero position, where they would blend into the contour of the wings. The hydraulic system would require thirteen seconds to retract the flaps fully. Retraction of flaps lessens the wings' resistance to the air, reducing lift. This causes a plane to pause in its climb. But its speed increases because of the elimination of the flaps' drag, and the speed makes up for the loss of lift. In a heavily loaded plane, however, the pause may stretch into prolonged level flight until the plane can build up enough speed to climb again. With an exceptionally heavy load, a plane may even lose some altitude before resuming its climb. If it cannot build up the necessary speed, however, it may continue to lose altitude until it hits the ground.

Captain Marsh noted that as his plane's speed increased to 130 and then 135 knots, the flaps were still retracting. When the needle reached 140 knots, he called out his last order for a normal take-off climb: "Meto." The single word, in aviation parlance, meant "maximum except take-off" power, and Andon began slowly to retard the four throttles. Like all maneuvers in the take-off, this was standard operating procedure in the DC-6. Operating a plane's engines at maximum power for more than two minutes may well burn them out.

Andon moved the four throttles together a fraction of an inch at a time, watching the manifold pressure on the four engines drop from 59½ inches to 50 inches. Then he reached forward to toggle the propellers from 2,800 r.p.m. to 2,600 r.p.m. With the flaps retracting and the power being reduced, the rate of climb fell from 800 feet per minute to 400. But this too was normal.

At the same time, Dixwell, with radio microphone in hand, acknowledged the tower's instructions to change frequency to tune in the radar departure controller. With a flip of the wrist he switched the radio channel selector, and then something made him turn in his seat to watch Andon reducing power. Perhaps that something was a slowness with which Andon, young and new at his job, was manipulating the throttles—a slowness which bothered Dixwell as a former chief pilot. Perhaps it was something else. Nevertheless, at a critical moment in the take-off, the first officer took his eyes from his flight instruments. He watched the flight engineer for several seconds. Then, something outside the front windshield caught his eye. What it was he did not know. But then he saw a mass of white coming up rapidly toward him, and he cried out.

"Al, ground!"

IN the La Guardia tower, Controller Goodman handed the dispatch sheet for Northeast Flight 823 to the radar departure controller, Michael McNamara. The radar man, seated at the radar set in the center of the darkened tower room, picked up the blip of Flight 823 as the DC-6 flew over the end of Runway 4, a quarter of a mile from the radar transmitter installation beside the runway. He intended to follow the flight approximately nineteen miles on the twenty-mile radar scope before transferring control to the 100-mile-range radar setup at the Air Route Control Center at Idlewild.

The thin white illuminating line of the radar set swept the scope every two seconds. In the quiet of the tower, with the voices of other controllers talking to planes a muted babble in the background, Mike McNamara calmly followed the radar blip of Flight 823 as it moved out from the center of the radar screen. He saw it the second time as the illuminated line swept the scope, and the third time. The blip moved straight away from Runway 4. On the fourth sweep of the radar arm, McNamara sat bolt upright. The blip had moved sharply to the left.

Never had he seen such a drastic departure from course on take-off. He raised his head to find Goodman, the watch supervisor. Then, disbelieving what he had seen, he turned back to the radar. The radar arm swept the scope. But there was no plane.

Inside the cabin, few sensed that the plane was turning and descending. Mrs. Blanche Zukowski, a devout Baptist, was still praying, with her eyes closed, "Thy kingdom come. Thy will be done . . ."

Peggy Williams, a Worcester girl going to visit her fiancé, who was a crop duster pilot in Florida, suddenly became aware that she was leaning forward against her seat belt rather than back in her chair. "What a funny feeling," she commented quietly. "This doesn't seem right at all."

Norman Davis, the former pilot, gazing out his window over the left wing, saw the white of the snow-covered ground change to the deep black of Flushing Bay. He saw patches of white in the water which he took for ice floes. Then he saw masses of white and he thought, Land again. No sooner had the thought occurred to him than he noticed the wing outside his window. It was almost perpendicular to the ground. He was astonished at so steep a bank, and equally surprised that he had felt no sensation of banking. In that instant he knew he was going to crash.

Farther back on the left side, Kenneth Kronen saw a straight row of trees coming up at him. He was so aghast he could say nothing to his wife, who was singing an improvised song to the child on her lap, "We're flying . . . we're flying . . . we're flying to Miami . . ."

Still farther back, in the last double seat on the left side, Mason Benson observed the snowflakes outside his window becoming larger and larger and larger.

Behind Mason, in the stewardess' jump seat, Emily

Gately thought she heard an explosion, like a car's backfire, in the extreme tail of the plane.

On the opposite side, Edwin Dresner, the building contractor, was holding his wife's hand for luck when he saw a large ball of bright orange flame fill a window across the aisle. It came from the location of No. 2 engine, the inboard one on the left side, but Dresner knew it was more than engine exhaust.

"Fire!" someone screamed.

"We're on fire!"

"The motor's on fire!"

"We're going to crash!"

"Fire!"

When Dixwell yelled, "Al, ground!" Captain Marsh jerked his head up, away from his instruments, and looked out the window. The ground was perhaps a hundred feet away, perhaps ten feet. He couldn't tell. But he could perceive that the plane was in a bank with the left wing down.

Instinctively, he pulled back hard on the wheel in a desperate effort to lift the plane, and simultaneously he rolled the wheel to the right to correct for the left bank.

The ground seen from the plane was Rikers Island, a grim patch of filled land one mile wide and a half-mile across, situated where the East River meets Flushing Bay. It was approximately one mile north of the tip of Runway 4. The island, as inaccessible as Alcatraz, contains five huge concrete buildings which constitute the Penitentiary of the City of New York. There some 2,500 men convicted of petty crimes and misdemeanors serve jail sentences up to three years.

Swooping down upon the island at almost 140 knots, the

plane slashed through a row of young trees—ironically enough, London plane trees—which were cultivated on the island for New York's parks and streets. Slicing off the tree tops some fifteen feet from the ground, the plane careened down a small hill. The left outboard propeller slashed the ground first. Then the left wing tip smashed into the ground. The plane bounced on the aft end of the fuselage, then the right wing tip struck 150 feet farther on.

With its landing gear still retracted, the plane skidded through the snow on its belly. The No. 1 and the No. 2 engines tore loose from the left wing. Then the entire left wing cracked off.

In the seconds that the plane began to disintegrate, the electrical system was severed, plunging the plane's interior into blackness darker than the night's. The exterior of the plane blazed a brilliant orange as the wing tanks, laden with three thousand gallons—or nine tons—of high-octane gasoline, were ignited by the shattered engines.

Yet this was not a severe crash. Captain Marsh's split-second, instinctive action had leveled the angle of impact. The slender trees had slowed the plane and the snow and mud on the small hill cushioned the final slide.

In the cockpit, the first impact seemed hardly worse than a rough normal landing. But Alva Marsh sat at his controls stunned. First there was utter blackness. Then the glow of fire reflected on the snow and glared on his windshield. The plane slid on and on and the men in the cockpit peered helplessly through the windshield awaiting the end.

The slide seemed eternal to Dixwell. Snow, slush, mud and twigs whipped against his windshield. Andon, perched on the engineer's jump seat behind the two pilots, was thrown violently forward against his seat belt. His right hand, still on the throttles he had been retarding, helped to support him as his left hand grasped the glare shield in front of him, and he braced himself for the final shock.

The incredible swiftness of events left no time for any man in the cockpit to do anything. No one tried to switch off the ignition in accordance with the procedure for avoiding fire. No one reached for the fire extinguishers. No one thought of the emergency flashlights on the cockpit walls.

The men sat there and the plane hurtled on through the snow, first smoothly, then more and more roughly until it bounced violently once or twice and came to a stop. As the plane jerked to a halt, the entire tail section snapped off aft of the pressure bulkhead which separated it from the passenger cabin. The tail fin came to rest bolt upright, twenty-nine feet high, like a severed limb in the swirling snow, just eight feet to the left of the body of the plane. Three hundred feet away was the southernmost concrete building of the prison.

Perhaps the one stroke of luck in this luckless flight was that, of all of congested New York City, the plane came to rest on the flat, soft ground of a vegetable patch. A half-mile in any direction and Flight 823 to Miami would have come down in dark, icy water. One hundred yards ahead, it would have crumpled against the concrete prison. And if it had struck with its wing perpendicular to the ground, as it almost did, it would have cartwheeled to total destruction.

Instead, when it did stop, every one of the 101 men, women and children aboard was alive.

Captain Marsh unhooked his safety belt and jumped to his feet. Whirling around, he looked through the open top half of the Dutch door behind the cockpit. With a view of about three-quarters of the cabin, he saw thick black smoke, flicks of fire and his passengers standing in the aisle in utter confusion. To go back there and try to restore order, he knew would be senseless. The best thing he and his crew could do, he thought, was to get the emergency exits open from outside.

As a strong odor of smoke wafted into the cockpit, Al Marsh turned to his co-pilot and engineer. "Let's get out of here," he shouted, reaching for the sliding window near his seat.

Chapter Nine

IN escaping from a burning airplane, there is little time for that fine tradition of the sea: women and children first. There is so little time at all. . . .

Captain Marsh, having given his evacuation order to his crew, slid open his side window and leaped five or six feet to the ground. Dixwell tugged at his side window but found it jammed. He scrambled across the two pilot arm-chairs and followed Marsh out the captain's window. Andon found his quickest exit to be the cockpit crew door behind and to the right of his seat. Flinging the door open, he stared at the fire on the right wing. The heat drove him back. He looked around. He saw chaos in the passenger cabin behind him. He saw smoke rolling thickly toward the cockpit. He saw flashes of flame and heard the screams and cries of the people inside. His duties as flight engineer, he knew, called for him to go back into the cabin to help the stewardesses evacuate passengers. But he knew too the futility of trying to quell panic inside a black and smoke-filled cabin. Better, he thought, to try to open an exit door from the outside and help people out that way. His decision came in a flash—as it had for the others in the cockpit—and Andon turned back to the crew door. He took one last look about the cockpit and, seeing that it was empty, went to the door and jumped.

Inside the cabin, ninety-five passengers and three stewardesses suddenly and acutely faced the prospect of dying.

They had had no warning. The stewardesses had been trained to prepare passengers for a crash, to station ablebodied men at each emergency exit, to prepare life rafts and life jackets if the plane were over water. But all this presupposed an emergency at high altitude, not a sudden disaster close to the ground.

The impact of the crash had been so mild that it failed to set off the emergency lights which are powered by batteries and designed to illuminate the ten emergency exits when there is a jolt harder than a normal landing. None of the exits was lighted when the short circuiting of the electrical system plunged the cabin into darkness.

Through holes torn in the plane's skin, flames from the left wing's gasoline tanks shot into the middle of the cabin and roared toward the tail like a blast from a military flame thrower. Acrid smoke billowed in the closed quarters and while the flames shot rearwards, the smoke poured forward.

In the first row of triple seats, Arthur and Mary Bourgoin shielded their heads with their arms. While the plane slid through the snow, they heard the wooden partition in front of them split and splinter with an awesome crunch. Arthur Bourgoin, in the middle seat, clambered over the woman in the window seat to the emergency door at their right. The door was closed but the window had jarred open.

Breathing in smoke and suddenly aware that she might die, his twenty-seven-year-old wife thought first, not of her young daughter at home or of the child in her womb, but of her mother. My poor mother . . . when she reads the *Daily Kennebec Journal* . . . she thought. Then she looked to her right and saw her husband's feet disappearing out the window. Mary Bourgoin also climbed over the elderly woman in the window seat to follow her husband. Her eyes met those of the older woman. It was a moment that stood still in time. Then Mary Bourgoin was at the window and saw her husband lying in the snow. He called to her, "Jump, jump." She jumped, and she and her husband ran from the burning plane, believing that they would be the only survivors.

The front of a plane usually bears the brunt of a crash. But those in the forward section of this plane were more fortunate than those in the rear. They had smoke, rather than fire, to contend with. Across the aisle from the Bourgoins, in the second row of double seats, Gerry Lassell, the Northeast instrument mechanic, thought of his twenty-one-year-old wife and not of his young son. When the plane rumbled to a stop, the young, thin man saw a jagged hole where the floor and wall met behind his seat. Pointing with outstretched arm, he yelled at his wife: "Go for the hole." She stumbled alone toward it. The jolt of the crash had flung their son, Roy, from her arms. The child bounced in the aisle and slid along the floor to the closed door of the buffet. Mrs. Reddington, in the first-row aisle seat, snatched the boy and followed her husband toward the same jagged hole, which gaped between seats 2 and 3 on the left. Gerry Lassell struggled to stand up in his seat which had been partly torn from its legs and tilted forward. But his seat belt, which he had looped around itself, held him fast. Finally remembering, he carefully unknotted the belt, unbuckled it and made for the hole.

It looked like a bear trap, and in its mouth it held a woman, half in and half out of the plane. Lassell placed his foot firmly on the woman's back and pushed her out, and then dived through the hole. His aim was perfect. He landed in the snow with only a minor cut on one hand. Only later did he discover that the woman he had pushed was his wife. In her violent exit, the jagged metal had deeply gashed her upper arm. Once he realized he was safe, Lassell turned back to the plane to help others.

In the second-row aisle seat, across from where Lassell had been sitting, Mrs. Zukowski had been still intoning the Lord's Prayer when the plane hit. "We'll all be killed," she screamed. Freeing herself from her seat belt, she saw a crowd at an opening ahead of her on the right side of the plane. She would never get out that way, she thought. Cupping her hand over her nose and mouth against the smoke, she tried to fight her way to a hole she could see across the aisle.

The small, dark-complexioned Worcester woman got across the crowded aisle, but tripped and fell not far from the opening. Repeatedly she tried to rise, but each time someone trampled her. For months afterwards she would bear the imprint of a man's shoe on her back. Mrs. Zukowski told herself, "Gosh, I'm going to burn to death." Then she realized that she no longer was being trampled and that all was quiet around her. She was alone.

She crawled to the gap between seats 2 and 3 and sensed the fresh, moistly chill air outside. She rose to her feet to climb out, but a cloud of smoke enveloped her head. She collapsed, falling backward. Semiconscious, she inched her way on her back toward the hole. "Please, God," she prayed, "don't let me burn to death." She thought she saw her Lord's face in the fire.

Outside, Gerry Lassell saw a pair of legs dangling through the jagged hole. He ran to them and pulled. Mrs. Zukowski tumbled out. Lassell and another man dragged her away from the burning plane. Partially revived, she again visualized her Lord's countenance filling the sky beyond the bright orange of the fire. "God, you saved me!" she cried, running through the snow.

The two stewardesses seated amidship, facing the rear, started for the exit doors before the plane stopped sliding. Kay Virchow had felt the plane tilt to the left but she had not known what it portended. She had sensed that the plane was climbing laboriously, then suddenly the feeling was gone. When the plane hit the ground, she heard what sounded like an explosion and at the same time heard passengers cry out, "We're going to crash . . . the motor is on fire."

When the plane hit, she felt a wrench in her right shoulder. She was already unbuckling her seat belt. While the plane skidded along, she got to her feet and headed for the big main cabin door in front of her seat. "Get the exits," screamed Dottie Steele. Kay braced herself against the wall as the plane slid to a stop. She grasped the big handle of the cabin door and tried to open it. Two men quickly came to her side and helped her. But with all their tugging, they failed to budge the door which would have provided the largest exit. They struggled on, little knowing that the crash had deformed the shape of the plane and had jammed every door on the left side.

On the other side, however, Benjamin Opatowski jerked down the handle to the emergency door at his side with such vehemence that the handle snapped off. But the door opened over the right wing and the sixty-two-year-old baker, dragging his wife behind him, leaped out of the plane. It was the only door opened in the passenger cabin.

Kay Virchow, abandoning the main cabin door, groped along the burning wall on the left side and tried to open the first window she came to, but it was not an emergency exit. She could not open the next one either. All about her was chaos. The plane was filling with smoke. The twenty-six-year-old stewardess saw flames streaking down the walls from the middle of the cabin to the tail. Through the bedlam, she heard Dottie Steele calling out, "Over here, folks . . . this way out . . . over here . . ."

Kay pushed her way through the passengers standing in the aisle and found on the right side, not far from Dottie Steele, another opening. Now she too began calling, "Over here, over here."

She had to force some passengers to jump down onto the flaming right wing so that they could roll off to the ground. Other passengers nearby did not respond to her call; like horses afraid to leave a burning barn, they preferred the familiarity of their seats to the unknown. Kay Virchow returned to the center aisle to lead out as many as she could.

Gloria Chadwick, sitting in the aisle seat alongside the Opatowskis, did not lose her presence of mind. She quickly flung her coat, which she had had on her lap, over her head to protect herself from the fire. Then, sensing that she had survived the crash, she helped push the elderly Opatowskis toward the open door near their triple seat. She turned back into the plane to seek her mother and father, but the press of other passengers toward the open exit blocked her way. She yielded to follow the throng out the door, hoping that she could somehow reach her parents from the outside.

Mrs. Chopelas, the five-foot-three Malden mother who had been so afraid of flying, now mustered the toughness developed in raising seventeen children and caring for a sixteen-room Victorian house. She had no trouble with her seat belt because she had not fastened it. Clasping her little boy to her bosom, she climbed over the woman sitting immobile in the aisle seat. Her neighbor at the window seat also appeared to be unconscious or dead, but Mrs. Chopelas had herself and her son to worry about. In her singleminded determination, she left her mink coat behind her in the seat and pushed her way down the aisle. Clad only in a low-cut green taffeta dress, she was being severely burned, but she was unaware of pain.

She sensed that she was stepping on people who had fallen, but she told herself, "It's them or me . . ." As she approached an emergency door, she saw Dottie Steele and she breathed in the chill air. "I'm going to live," she exulted. But at the threshold, her determination failed her. "Jump!" the stewardess yelled, but Mrs. Chopelas saw the flames raging outside and she backed away. "Jump!" Dottie shouted again. Mrs. Chopelas could not. Dottie Steele took Gregory from her and tossed him out the door so that he would clear the trailing edge of the wing. Mrs. Chopelas still hung back; then someone behind her propelled her forward, through the door and to safety.

Mindy Sanger, who was three and a half years old, sat quietly in her aisle seat by the right wing, still munching her sandwich when the plane struck. At her side, her mother, Joan Sanger, a tall, well-built young matron, was stunned for a second that seemed as long as eternity. But when she became aware of the flames engulfing the right wing outside her window, she sprang to action. She whipped off her seat belt and Mindy's. The child was still chewing her sandwich. Mrs. Sanger held open her jacket. "Put your head in here," she told her daughter, and picking her up, she joined the throng in the center aisle. The woman in the window seat, who had taken a sleeping pill before take-off, appeared to be still dozing.

In the aisle, Mrs. Sanger fought to keep on her feet against the pushing and shoving. If she fell, she told herself, it would be the end. The acrid smoke already was constricting her throat and lungs. Reaching the hole in the right side of the fuselage over the wing, Mrs. Sanger found her way blocked. A woman was stuck in the hole. Telling Mindy to ride piggy-back, Mrs. Sanger used her freed hands to push the woman out. The woman's foot caught in the ragged edge of the hole, and Mrs. Sanger struggled desperately to disentangle it. Finally, the woman tumbled to the wing and slid to the ground. Then, with the uncomplaining Mindy on her back, Mrs. Sanger crawled through the hole, carefully picked her way down the wing and jumped to the snow.

She sat there until voices penetrated her daze. "Get away from the plane . . . it's going to explode . . ." Stumbling to her feet, she faced a wall of fire in the snow surrounding the plane. Then she walked through the fire, half carrying and half dragging her daughter.

Mrs. Barbara Domash, a petite mother from Plainview, Long Island, struggled against the crowd and smoky fumes, holding her eleven-month-old son, William, on one arm, and her three-and-a-half-year-old daughter, Eileen, on the other.

As she pushed her way along the aisle, the five-foot-three mother began to lose her hold on Eileen. The three-and-a-half-year-old grew heavier and heavier. By the time Mrs. Domash could see the emergency exit over the right wing, she was not carrying but dragging her screaming daughter. As she reached the exit, her grip was reduced to a grasp of the child's long brown curls, and in the final surge, she lost even that. Still clutching her son, she was thrust through the open door. Eileen remained in the plane.

To six-year-old Nancy Tulowiecki, still coloring the pictures in the book on her lap, the crash had felt like a roller coaster ride. She and her father were in seats 4A and 4B, ahead of the left wing. When the plane hit, Ed Tulowiecki, a former sailor, clutched his daughter with his left hand and with his right braced himself on the seat in front of him until the plane stopped. His first thought, seeing fire and smoke, was: Eddie, you lucky dog, going to confession and communion last week.

Grasping Nancy tightly by the hand, he made his way forward to the hole between seats 2A and 3A. In seconds, thick smoke blackened the inside of the plane up forward. Nearing the hole, Tulowiecki maneuvered his daughter in front of him and with his hands on her slender waist guided her to the opening.

Just as Nancy stooped to go out the hole, a man pushed her aside and crawled out ahead of her. But before he did, his eyes met those of Ed Tulowiecki. The glare of the fire outside lighted the man's face. It was a moment of truth, and Ed Tulowiecki is certain to this day that he would know that man's face anywhere, any time.

When the man had gone, Tulowiecki lifted his daughter and placed her at the edge of the hole. Then, with his foot, he thrust her as far from the plane as he could. After that, he jumped. In the snow, he grasped Nancy's hand and ran as fast as he could. Only later did he realize that through it all, Nancy, confident of her father, had neither cried out nor spoken a word.

The incalculable and the fortuitous govern men's lives. Most of those killed were seated in the rear of the plane in the path of the flames which shot into the cabin from a point near the rear edge of the left wing. Survival for many of those in the rear could well have depended upon whether they were inhaling or exhaling. One gulp of fire would have seared the lungs and caused instant death. One normal breathful of smoke would have brought unconsciousness, followed by asphyxiation in seconds.

When the No. 1 and No. 2 engines parted from the left wing, before the wing itself tore loose from the plane, they ripped open the wing's gasoline tanks and tore a hole in the fuselage near the wing's trailing edge. Fire blasted into the cabin as though propelled by a flame thrower, crossed to the right side of the plane, traveled down the center aisle and struck the triple seats on the right in the rear of the plane. Divergent flames flitted down the left wall like chain lightning.

Seated just ahead of the breach through which the fire shot into the cabin, Norman Davis was spared the worst of its heat. In the long seconds before the plane hit, he had known it would crash. He thought it would come down in Flushing Bay and he steeled himself for a cold swim.

The mild impact of the crash surprised him and he decided to wait until the plane stopped sliding before releasing his seat belt. He felt no fear, and his mind seemed singularly clear.

"Come on, let's go," he said to his blond seat companion. Davis had been thinking of an exit door in front of his seat, but when the plane came to a stop, he saw the window of the door engulfed in flames and decided to try the opposite side of the plane.

"I can't move," the girl beside him cried.

Davis unfastened her seat belt, and in the aisle, the girl wrapped her arms around his waist, and hugging close, literally followed in his footsteps.

Moving down the aisle, Davis stopped where he remembered a stewardess had said there was a life raft. Still thinking the plane had come down in water, he reached overhead to a locker in the ceiling and tried desperately to get at the life raft inside. But as the crowd pushed on, he gave up and decided to brave the water without raft or life jacket.

As smoke began to stifle him, he put his handkerchief over his nose and mouth. "Can I have your handkerchief?" the girl pleaded. Davis passed it back to her, and she put it to her eyes to wipe away the smarting flow of mascara.

The open emergency door at the end of the right wing seemed walled off by fire when Davis reached it. Through the flames, he could see people on the ground below. The fire ahead of him seemed less menacing than the smoke and fumes behind him.

"Hang on!" he told the girl, who probably never thought of letting go. He waited an instant and jumped to the wing beneath the door. Then seeing another wall of flames at the edge of the wing, he waited for a break and leaped, with his companion on his back. He had the impression that they were flying through the air. They landed in a heap and rolled over. Looking back at the wing, Davis saw a man afire jumping.

"Roll in the snow," Davis screamed. The man rolled over and over, the flames flickered out, and the man staggered away.

Kenneth Kronen, in the window seat by the trailing edge of the left wing, probably was the first to feel the inward blast of flames. His hair and his ears felt as though they were burning. When the searing heat hit his face, he threw up his hands to protect it and then his hands felt afire. Strapped to his seat, he thought, I'm a goner.

While he sat stunned, his pretty wife galvanized herself into action. She whipped off her seat belt and groped on the floor for her son, Ricky, who had fallen from her lap. In the blackness, she found the boy and began to reach desperately along the wall for the handle of the emergency door which, she remembered, was beside the seat in front of hers. The wall was hot. She realized her hands were being burned but, at whatever cost, she knew she had to reach that door.

She could not find the handle and it occurred to her that if she did find it, she would not know how to turn it. She resented, briefly, that the operation of the emergency doors had not been explained before take-off. Actually, all emergency exits on planes are designed to spring open when the handle is pressed downward.

Failing to find the handle, Mrs. Kronen stumbled out into the aisle, shouting to her husband, "Hurry up, hurry up." Kenneth Kronen, awakening to reality, ripped off his seat belt, grasped his wailing six-week-old son from the floor and fought his way into the confusion in the aisle. In the darkness, he could not find his wife.

Mrs. Kronen, ahead of him, gulped smoke. She felt as though the inside of her body were afire. I'm going to die, she thought, and she prayed that death would come quickly. Then she spotted the light of a fire glowing through the hole in the right side of the plane. Hope resurged. "I'm going to live ... to live," she told herself again and again as she moved resolutely toward the glow.

Coming into Runway 4, La Guardia Airport, on the front approach, from 250 feet

Control tower, La Guardia Airport (radar man on the right)

Aerial view of La Guardia Airport from 6,000 feet, showing Runway 4, Rikers Island to the left, Whitestone Bridge in the background

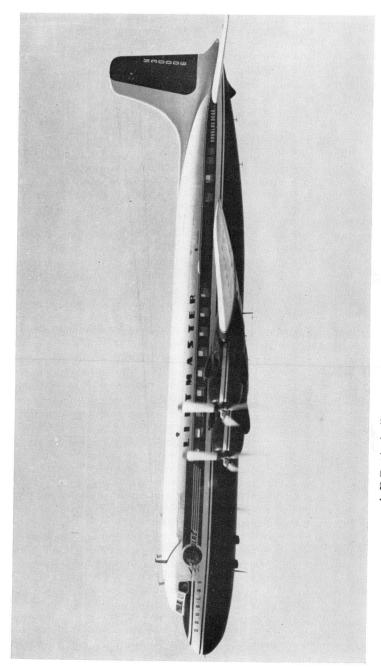

A DC-6A similar to the one that crashed on Rikers Island

Captain Alva V. R. Marsh, during
World War II

Co-pilot Basil S. Dixwell

Stewardess Emily Gately

Stewardess Kay Virchow

Peggy and Mason Benson

Mrs. Blanche Zukowski

Arthur and Mary Bourgoin

DC-6A N34953 INSTRUMENT PANEL

1. altimeter
2. zero reader
3. air speed
4. course indicator
5. deviation indicator
6. artificial horizon
7. dual ADF
8. turn & bank
9. C-2A gyrosyn compass
10. rate of climb
11. deviation indicator
12. BMEP (Brake Mean Effective Pressure)
13. manifold pressure gauges (4 pointers in 2 instruments)
14. engine RPM (4 pointers in 2 instruments)
15. cylinder head temperature gauges (4 pointers in 2 instruments)
16. fuel flow gauges (4 pointers in 2 instruments)
17. wing flaps position indicator
18. outside ("free") air temperature
19. water (ADI) pump pressure gauges (4 pointers in 2 instruments)
20. fuel pressure gauges (4 pointers in 2 instruments)
21. oil pressure gauges (4 pointers in 2 instruments)

(George Van Photos, Newark)

SIMILAR TO N34954

22. oil temperature gauges (4 pointers in 2 instruments)
23. carburetor air temperature gauges (4 pointers in 2 instruments)
24. cabin and airfoil anti-icing heater control panel
25. landing light switches
26. engine cowl flap controls
27. engine supercharger controls
28. magnetic compass
29. compass
30. zero reader selector switch
31. check list (illuminated scroll)

32. engine fire warning and CO_2 selector handles
33. left-hand CO_2 discharge handle
34. V_1-V_2 speed chart
35. rudder pedal
36. throttles
37. throttle lock
38. prop control box
39. nose wheel steering
40. elevator trim tab
41. ADF tuning panel
42. auto pilot
43. VHF nav. tuning panel
44. ADF tuning panel

Laura and Norman Chadwick

Gloria Chadwick

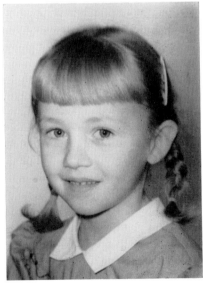

Edward Tulowiecki

Nancy Tulowiecki

Captain Marsh soon after the crash

Flight Engineer Angelo Andon and Captain Marsh on ferryboat

Co-pilot Dixwell in ambulance

Captain Marsh testifying at CAB hearing

The crumpled nose, soon after the crash

Firemen searching the wreckage in the snowstorm

Stewardess Doris Steele being carried away

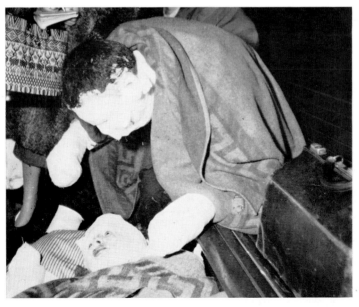

Mason Benson bending over his wife on the way to a hospital

The prison chaplain in prayer for the dead, lying in the foreground (N. Y. DAILY NEWS PHOTO)

Aerial view of the crash the following morning, with New York City Penitentiary in the background

CAB men and police in search of clues (N. Y. DAILY NEWS PHOTO)
(*insert*) Joseph O. Fluet, CAB investigator-in-charge

CAB men searching the wreckage; a passenger's travel clock
in foreground

Eugene Searle (center) and two other CAB investigators
examining the innards of the plane (N. Y. DAILY NEWS PHOTO)

Five or six persons were ahead of her, moving, oh, so slowly. She remembered what people have been known to do to save their own lives and their children's. Despite the child in her arms, Mrs. Kronen could not bring herself even to push the strangers in front of her. She waited her turn, pleading, "Hurry, please hurry . . ."

With her son Ricky straddling her stomach, Mrs. Kronen gingerly climbed feet first out of the hole, dropped to the wing and then, still clutching her boy, slid to the ground.

Her husband found his way to the emergency exit farther aft on the right side, tossed his infant son Mark to the ground and jumped after him—without consciously knowing what he was doing.

In the seat in front of the Kronens', and also in the path of the thrusting flames, Dr. Kovnat, the dentist, leaped to his feet and cried out, "I'm burning, I'm burning . . . my God, I'm burning." He tried to rush to the aisle, but he could not get by his brother-in-law in the aisle seat.

Dr. Taub, still in a state of shock, struggled to stand up to escape the intense heat he felt on the back of his neck. But he was still strapped to his seat and the harder he pushed against the seat belt to escape the fire behind him, the tighter the belt became. It was designed to withstand precisely this kind of forward pressure. After a moment of frantic struggle, Dr. Taub suddenly realized his situation: to release the seat belt and avert burning to death, he would have to sink back into the seat and expose himself to another ordeal of fire.

In that moment of clarity, the choice was obvious. He leaned back, thrust his head toward the flames, and freed himself. The two middle-aged men pushed out into the aisle. But once there, they stood still in the black confusion of the crowd, knowing neither where to go nor what to do.

For seconds, in the smoke and heat, they cursed aloud their stupidity in not having quit the plane before take-off. Dr. Taub, with a feeling of detachment, heard himself shout, "Good-by, Ben, this is it . . ." Acutely aware of everything, he felt quite objective. He accepted without panic what he expected to happen and he wondered how long it would be before he lost consciousness. Would he feel those searing pains of burning again before the end?

Resigned and preoccupied, Dr. Taub suddenly became aware that two passengers who had been crowding him on his right had disappeared. Looking in that direction, he saw an opening in the side of the plane. He rushed to it and found an emergency door. It was still closed but its window had been knocked out. Pushing his head out, he breathed fresh air. He turned back into the plane and shouted, "Ben, follow me." He eased himself headfirst out the window and slid, hands outstretched, along the outside of the burning plane. A moment later his brother-in-law, with his trousers afire, landed in the snow beside him.

In the tail section, where so many lost their lives, Mason Benson insisted to himself, "This can't be happening to me." To Benson, the plane had seemed to strike the ground with a thud, followed almost immediately by the loudest bang he had ever heard. The reverberation made him think he was inside a tin can that was being pounded from outside.

The impact tore Benson's seat from its tracks and catapulted it, with him in it, into the aisle two seats forward. The tall athlete landed on his right shoulder and arm. He looked up from the floor and saw bright orange flame, like the blast of a great furnace, shooting toward him from up front. He ducked his head into his arms and felt the intense, stabbing heat pass just above him.

God, it's hot in here, he thought as smoke began to filter down to the floor. If I have to go, let me go in comfort.

Choking on smoke and acting more by instinct than by reason, Mason Benson unstrapped his seat belt and groped his way back to his wife, calling, "Peggy . . ."

"Here," she answered in the blackness.

Feeling his way, he touched her thigh. He helped his wife up and then he remembered the emergency window by her seat. The directions he had memorized came to mind: "Pull up, push in and push window out." He groped along the wall. Despite its heat, he felt no pain, and somehow he found the two finger holes by which he could release the window.

The ground appeared to be about fifteen feet below and Peggy Benson, crouched at the window ledge, hesitated until her husband pushed her out.

Like many others in the plane, Benson had acted instinctively. Shock had blocked off hearing and feeling. He was unaware of the confusion, the shouts, the screams about him. He realized there was fire, but he was oblivious to the searing of his own flesh.

Before leaving the plane, Benson turned and saw, leaning against the seat his wife had occupied, the figure of the young stewardess who had been sitting behind them.

Emily Gately thought she heard an explosion in the tail just before the plane struck the ground. She sat dazed, her eyes shut, as the plane slid to a stop. This is it, she thought. Those who fly for a living are seldom without some degree of subconscious dread. The young stewardess began to pray. But her inactivity was momentary. Freeing herself from her seat belt, she noticed a mass of people gathered about a small hole in the right side of the fuselage in the rear. There were so many of them that she began to look for another means of escape. Not having been trained on a DC-6, she did not know where the emergency exits were. She beat on a window with the heel of a shoe.

Mason Benson reached forward, grasped her and pushed her slim body out the small window in front of him. Then he turned to where he had seen two men, but he felt that he was about to faint from the heat. He turned back and dived through the window.

Across the aisle from the Bensons and two seats forward, Charles Naylor counted the bumps when the plane crashed: BUMP BUMP-BUMP. He was tossed in his seat: RIGHT LEFT-RIGHT. As the plane bounced and slid, the young pianist whipped off his seat belt and stood up just as the blast of fire swept down the cabin. He saw it coming but could do nothing. The flame hit him in the face. He cupped his hand over his mouth and nose in anguish.

The rear of the cabin filled with orange flame. But one spot of dark gray appeared to Naylor's right and he leaped for it through the flame without any assurance he would find a way out of the plane. He thrust his hand into the spot of gray and found it to be an open window, which probably had been blown out by the heat.

Unable to get through the small opening, Naylor thrust his arms out. Bending his elbows, he forced back the molten metal to enlarge the opening and dived out. In the snow, he scrambled to his feet and ran through two rings of blazing gasoline until he was forty or fifty feet from the plane. Then he remembered his wife.

Inside the plane, aware that she was beginning to breathe smoke, Mrs. Naylor prepared to die. She had no idea that her husband was not sitting there beside her, but she too saw a "little gray thing" in the fire and she moved in a daze toward the window.

To Charles Naylor outside, the burning plane looked like a prop in a Hollywood spectacular. It appeared intact, gleaming white, with flames shooting into the black night air. Charles Naylor ran back through the rings of flames.

Through the window he saw his wife's red cashmere coat. Then he saw his wife, her head out, crying, "Charlie, Charlie."

Naylor pushed his wife's head back into the plane and shouted to her to put an arm through the window, then her head. She did and he seized her arm and pulled her out.

Outside, Gloria Chadwick searched and called out for her mother and father, all the while helping strangers who tumbled out of the open door by the trailing edge of the right wing. Finally, she made her way toward the tail of the plane and recognized her mother trying to crawl out of a hole in the side of the fuselage. The young skiing enthusiast and athlete ran to her mother's side and helped drag her out of the hole and away from the burning plane. Mrs. Chadwick, badly burned, sobbed that all who had been behind her inside the plane were trapped by the flames. The mother and daughter each knew that Norman Chadwick could not have escaped, yet they searched among the survivors in the snow for him.

Meanwhile, Andon had landed in the snow on all fours. Rising to his feet, he sighted a woman lying in the snow and stumbled toward her. Fearing the plane might explode at any moment, he grasped her hands and dragged her to safety. On the way, he passed another woman lying in the snow, so he returned to help her.

Captain Marsh, neither burned nor hurt when he jumped from the cockpit, was stunned by the suddenness of the catastrophe. Recovering his senses, he noticed the tall structure of the prison and mistook it for an apartment house. He thought he must be somewhere in the Bronx. The wilderness of the island puzzled him, as it did many of the survivors. But he could not dwell long on the anomaly. There were so many things to be done.

Heading for an emergency door over the left wing, Captain Marsh ran alongside the plane, but he found fire and no wing. Just forward of where the wing should have been, he came upon a jagged hole in the fuselage, through which people were pouring. He threw himself into helping survivors get clear of the plane.

Dixwell, after following the captain out the window, ran around the plane's nose to the right side, where he came upon passengers streaming through an opening over the flaming right wing, and he began to direct survivors away from the blazing plane.

In all, eighty-one men, women and children escaped. They did so within two minutes of the time the DC-6 stopped sliding.

THE snow-flecked windows of the La Guardia control tower suddenly were illuminated by a flash of orange. The glare came from beyond the end of Runway 4 and for a moment seemed to fill the sky.

John McNamara had just turned to report the disappearance of the radar blip of Northeast Flight 823 to his supervisor, Herbert Goodman, when the flash of light bathed the control room. The two men for a moment gazed silently at one another; the fear ever-latent in the hearts of men who direct plane movements had become reality.

"Northeast Eight-Twenty-Three," McNamara called sharply into his microphone. "La Guardia Departure Control at eighteen-zero-three [6:03 P.M.] ... correction on the time, eighteen-zero-two now ... Do you read La Guardia Departure one two zero point four [frequency] ... do you read?"

Correcting his reading of the wall clock lest he had made an error which later might be viewed as important, McNamara repeated his message. Meanwhile, Goodman summoned the plane on his own radio frequency. There was no reply. Incoming flights continued to report in to the tower.

Chapter
Ten

Goodman quickly cleared two planes for landing while still trying to make contact with Northeast 823.

The Eastern Airlines Martin 404, waiting to go after Al Marsh's plane, reminded the tower it was in the number one position for take-off. Goodman told it: "We are unable to work with aircraft that proceeded before you and we did see a red flash. . . . We don't know what it is. We're trying to determine what became of the aircraft."

"Okay."

Two more planes asked for take-off clearance and Goodman, wanting to keep all radio facilities clear for the missing plane, ordered:

"All aircraft stand by!"

Meanwhile, McNamara reported the Northeast flight to the Idlewild Control Center as a radio failure. This was, in the tradition of tower men, the conservative approach. The glow in the sky might be totally unrelated to the silence of Northeast 823, which could have become a radio failure.

But messages buzzed through the air with an intensity full of foreboding.

LA GUARDIA TOWER: New York, have you heard from Northeast Eight-Two-Three yet?

N. Y. CONTROL CENTER: No, I understand he's a radio failure.

LA GUARDIA TOWER: Well, I don't know if he's a radio failure or what. We haven't seen him on radar after he departed the runway. . . . Something may have happened to him.

N. Y. CONTROL CENTER: Okay, I'll see if I can find out something.

At Idlewild Control Center, three operators were put to work to attempt radio contact with the missing plane.

On the possibility that the crew had tuned to the wrong frequency, the three men worked different radio bands to call the plane repeatedly: "Northeast Eight-Two-Three, Northeast Eight-Two-Three, New York Center . . . do you read?"

Northeast's operations office at La Guardia was notified and it too joined in the radio search. Two airliners approaching La Guardia were requested to attempt contact with the missing plane. The Coast Guard Rescue Co-ordination Center was informed and asked to start a search, and Fletcher Brown, Coast Guard pilot on duty at Floyd Bennett Field in Brooklyn, took off in a warmed-up helicopter. A police launch docked in the East River was informed by radio. Herbert Goodman took from his desk drawer a list of agencies and men to be notified in an emergency and began to make telephone calls.

Down on the field at La Guardia, Donald Sullivan, maintenance manager of Butler Aviation, had seen the flash of orange in the sky as he faced north outside the Butler service hangar. It was reminiscent of his Air Force days in World War II, and he realized immediately that a plane had crashed.

Inside the Butler operations office, John J. Moran, operations supervisor, and Herbert Tagg, operations attendant, also saw the flash. They ran to a car and raced to the northern edge of the airfield. Atop the dike at Flushing Bay they looked out across the Rikers Island Channel. In the distance, through the snow flurries, rain and fog, they could see two small fires. On the car radio they notified the tower.

On Rikers Island, a middle-aged housewife placidly preparing her family dinner saw a fiery glow light her kitchen like a rising sun, and she thought of Armageddon. Mrs.

Marianne Proelss, wife of the Protestant chaplain of the prison, rushed to the door and flung it open. A bolt of flame cartwheeled low above the ground directly toward her. But it fell to the ground before it reached her. Having envisioned the end of everything, Mrs. Proelss was relieved. "It's only a plane," she told herself. Her houseboy, an inmate who had been helping her prepare dinner, cried, "There must be people who need help." He donned snow boots, grabbed his coat from a doorknob and dashed out. Mrs. Proelss handed him a flashlight.

The first thought of her son, Mike, a college student, was that an atomic bomb had fallen nearby. He ran upstairs to determine whether his younger sister was safe. Then he saw the burning plane and he followed the houseboy out into the snow.

The Reverend E. Frederick Proelss was lying in bed preparing his Sunday sermon when his thoughts were interrupted by a strange, whistling noise. He looked out a window just as the plane's left wing came off and burned, its fire eerily lighting the night. Using the phone on his desk, he called the prison central desk. "Emergency!" he cried. "A plane's crashed on the island." By the time he had dressed and hurried past his wife and young daughter at the kitchen door, survivors were stumbling toward the Protestant Mission House.

Among them the chaplain encountered an elderly man who leaned on his arm, exhausted, and remarked, "How fragile is life. If we only knew how close to death we are, we would all be a little kinder to each other."

In the house next to the Protestant Mission, the Reverend Anthony Glaser, S.J., the prison's Roman Catholic chaplain, looked out his window at the burning fragments of the plane and raised his hand in absolution for the victims.

From the prison blocks, inmates stared in horrified fascination at the blazing plane and human beings stumbling, crawling, running, or rolling in the snow to extinguish the fire which clung to their clothing. A high wind whipped and swirled the falling snow about the scene.

In command of the prison island that night was Deputy Warden James Harrison, a soft-spoken forty-nine-year-old Negro who once had worked as a subway conductor, had attended classes at Morehouse College and the City College of New York in his spare time, and had worked his way up to deputy warden during twenty years' service in the Correction Department.

Warden Harrison was jolted out of his routine by the explosion as he walked toward the prison's central desk in the main administration building. He ran to a window and, gazing upon the brightest light he had ever seen, he knew a plane had crashed. Living in the shadows of the thousands of planes that used La Guardia Airport, everyone who worked on the island had feared precisely that.

Warden Harry Silberglitt was away from the island for the day and Deputy Warden Harrison was faced with perhaps the most difficult decision of his career. He had only twenty-eight officers on duty. But he did have sixty-nine inmates assigned to the transportation gang and the farm gang who had been ordered an hour before to be ready to start clearing snow from the walks after dinner. Should he use the prisoners in rescue work and risk their escape in the confusion? Or, even worse, risk their being killed or injured?

"Get the gangs who are ready for snow clearing," Harrison shouted to Ray Shanahan, the officer at the desk.

"There are no officers to send with them," cried Shanahan.

"Just send them out," Harrison called back.

Directing one prison officer to turn on all the outdoor floodlights and another to alert the police and fire departments on the mainland, Harrison dashed out to the burning plane.

Throughout the small island community, men and women reacted to the plane crash with alacrity. From the prison hospital, one block beyond the administration building, Nurse Cecilia Moran hurried to the scene. The prison's medical supervisor, Dr. Meyer Farbman, left his house near the island's dock and raced for the hospital's medical supplies. Two nurses joined him. Assistant Deputy Warden Emil Joehnk, in charge of maintenance and transportation, telephoned the garage and told an inmate, who had risked censure by answering the telephone, to get ready the island's one fire engine pumper. The pumper had been delivered to the island four days before by the city fire department because the prison island was being temporarily cut off from all vehicles on the mainland during repairs to the Rikers ferry dock at East 134th Street in the Bronx.

The Protestant minister's houseman was the only prison inmate known to have reached the airplane in time to help survivors out. The conflagration seemed to tower two stories high and the houseman panicked for a moment. But, espying a woman struggling out of a hole in the fuselage, he ran to the plane, dragged her out and rolled her in the snow to douse her smoldering coat. A stout, elderly woman, she was unconscious or dead when he left her at a safe distance from the fire. He ran back to help someone who stuck half in and half out of the hole. It was a man, horribly burned about the face and hands. The houseman dragged the man alongside the elderly woman.

By that time, there were swarms of survivors all around, crying, "Where should we go? . . . What should we do? . . ." The houseman ran to one to whom others seemed to be looking for leadership, and pointed to the light shining from the mission house kitchen. "Go there . . . there's help there. . . ."

As the little group started away, the houseman turned back to the plane and came upon a stewardess limping aimlessly in the snow, clutching a small child.

He told her to give him the boy and to lean on him and he would take them to safety. "I don't need help," the young woman cried, stumbling on. "Go, help the others."

It was obvious that she was in shock. The inmate tried to lead her to the mission house, but she tried to fight him off, babbling that she had to go back to the plane and save the people inside. Then her legs gave way and she sagged to the ground. At this point, Mike Proelss, the chaplain's son, arrived. The two men lifted the stewardess, who was still clutching the child, and carried her to the Protestant Mission House.

In the mission house dining room, the college student and prisoner got their first full look at the stewardess. Her face was burned from forehead to neck. Her hair was singed almost to the roots. The skin was gone from her hands. Her shoes were gone, and her legs were burned to her thighs. But she pleaded to be allowed to return to the plane. The two men had to persuade her to stay put as an example to the others in the mission house.

The house soon filled with survivors. They occupied the chairs and couches in the living room, the dining room and the small front porch. Some stretched out on the floor, others wandered about in various stages of shock.

When Charles Naylor and his wife reached the house, they were surpised to find so many other survivors. Tramping through the snow, they had thought they alone had escaped.

In the kitchen, they extended their mutilated hands in supplication for first aid. Mrs. Naylor wept hysterically for her husband, explaining to all who would listen that he was a concert pianist. He needed his hands . . . his hands were his life. . . . She was unaware of the extent of her own injuries.

Naylor feared that his career had ended just when he had attained success. It seemed a cruel stroke of fate. Skin hung from his fingers like gray spider webs, and from his face and the face of his wife. To the horrified houseman, they looked as if they were wearing wax masks which were melting in the heat. The prisoner led them to the main administration building where the doctor had set up a first-aid station.

The houseman returned from the administration building with an armload of blankets for the people in the mission house. Mrs. Proelss moved about quietly, applying vaseline and ointment on burns. Dr. Taub walked around, calming the injured, explaining that he was a doctor and that even if he could not help them because of his own severely burned hands, he could see that they were being well cared for. John Nolan, the college sophomore, made his necktie a sling for one charred arm and helped himself to a kerchief from a woman passenger's head to make a sling for his other arm.

Norman Davis, who had seen the crash from its beginning, explored the mission house calmly until he came upon the chaplain's study where he found a telephone. The room was empty. Davis picked up the phone, dialed his home in Roslyn Heights, Long Island, and told his wife he was safe.

Other survivors straggled off from the burning plane in various directions, the more seriously injured following those less badly hurt. Several prisoners, who had been on snow-removal detail, directed them back to the main administration building. Many an inmate adopted a single survivor and tried to remain with him or her all through the ordeal of finding and receiving help.

Some passengers, once safely away from the plane, fell in the snow and sat or lay there dazed. Mrs. Barbara Domash rocked back and forth on the ground, clutching the baby she had saved and wailing for the daughter she had lost inside the airplane. Kenneth Kronen after a brief search found his five-week-old son where he had thrown him before he himself had jumped from the plane. Kronen paced up and down in the snow, holding his crying son in his arms while his burned hands hung limply from his wrists. He gave the baby to a prisoner who told him he was in no condition to care for it. Then, as part of a group of about twenty-five survivors, the Kronens were led by another inmate to the administration building.

"Are my ears still there?" he asked his wife.

"Yes," she replied, looking at his burned face. "Your ears are still there."

Others tramped about, peering into the agonized faces of survivors, looking for kinfolk. Gloria Chadwick and her mother searched the area in vain for the head of their family. Word got to Captain Marsh that the father of his friend Chief Stewardess Dorothy Richardson could not be found, and he too joined in the hunt.

Mrs. Esther Chopelas staggered toward the lights of a house in the distance, searching for two-and-a-half-year-old Gregory. She came upon one survivor and then another pleading for help, but she could not help them. In the home of Father Glaser, she collapsed, mercifully unaware of the extent of her own injuries. Her face had been virtually destroyed; parts of her hands, her legs, her back, her neck, had been burned severely. She was perhaps the most seriously injured of all the survivors.

But before she lapsed into unconsciousness, her son was brought to her and she saw that she had saved him: only a small portion of his right forearm had been burned. Later, when she was moved to the prison hospital, she was separated again from Gregory, and the boy reached the mainland as the only unidentified survivor. He could not give his name. He could only cry out, "Mommy . . . Mommy!"

While some survivors found their way to the chaplains' homes, and others were led to the administration building or the hospital, several wandered off in the direction in which the nose of the burning plane was pointing. Emily Gately walked through the snow in stockinged feet with the Bensons, thinking ingenuously: Gee, I came through this beautifully. . . . She was aware of the cold but she felt no pain from her burns. She was in shock.

The beautiful, red-haired Mrs. Benson, who also was severely burned, turned to her husband and said, "I feel faint, you'd better carry me." The six-foot-four athlete looked at his burned hands. He was aghast and for the first time pain registered in his numbed mind.

"I can't carry you," Benson told his wife. "You'd better keep walking, and don't turn around. Don't look back at the plane."

The glare of the fire lighted their way through what seemed a strange pastoral scene. Woods were all about and the dark of night was flecked with the beautiful white of falling snow. It was incongruous to the Bensons, for New York is a metropolis of skyscrapers housing eight million people.

After what seemed an endless trek, the three came on a long, low building off by itself. It was deserted. Mrs. Benson collapsed on a lone, small bench, and Emily Gately slumped into a straight-back chair. A sense of loneliness engulfed Mason Benson as he roamed around the quiet enclosure which was a chicken house unused in winter. Benson wondered whether he should go for help or just wait. The two women appeared comatose. On a small desk stood a telephone and Benson tried to use it, but his mangled hands would not obey. With an elbow, he knocked the phone from its cradle and bent down to listen. There was no dial tone. Painfully, he picked up a pencil from the desk, and clamping it between his teeth, tried to dial Operator. The phone was dead. Then, noticing on the desk a list of three digit telephone numbers for emergency, fire and internal offices, he dialed various combinations of three numbers, but could raise no one.

Others drifted into the chicken house. Mrs. Zukowski, her legs still bleeding from the gash she suffered when she was pulled through the jagged hole in the plane, staggered in and slumped into the one remaining chair. Gerry Lassell, who had saved her, arrived a little later, carrying his young son. His small blond wife was at his side. His light-colored suburban coat was smeared with Mrs. Zukowski's blood. Ed Tulowiecki, the Massachusetts garage owner, came in with his six-year-old daughter, Nancy. Neither had been seriously injured, but Nancy was troubled. "Oh, Daddy," she exclaimed, "my new pink dress will be all burned up." Several weary people smiled.

Mary and Arthur Bourgoin, who had thought they were the only survivors, were surprised to find some fifteen persons in the chicken house when they arrived after having wandered lost about the island. The young Maine housewife, who had had premonitions before this trip, tried to use the telephone. Having no success she put down the instrument. She was startled by a deep voice behind her. "You've got to keep trying. You've got your hands."

She turned to see a handsome, broad-shouldered man, who towered over everyone, peering at her through singed eyelashes. Mason Benson held out his hands with burned flesh hanging from his fingers. The sight has remained with Mary Bourgoin for years, but at that moment she turned back to the telephone and tried again and again, with no more success.

Gerry Lassell went about trying to help the seriously injured. Borrowing a necktie—he had not been wearing one—he tied a tourniquet above Mrs. Zukowski's bleeding right knee. Then, noticing a slim woman slumped in the other chair, he tucked one finger beneath her chin and lifted her face.

"Oh, my God!" he exclaimed. The face was grayish black, bereft of eyebrows and eyelashes, and topped by charred hair an inch or two long. Emily Gately heard the exclamation clearly and she wondered if her lipstick were smeared or her hair ruffled. She could not imagine what else was wrong, except that she felt so tired.

At the blazing wreck, Captain Marsh searched the left side for more survivors. He had pulled several passengers through the hole in the fuselage between the cockpit and left wing. But before long, the heat became so intense that he could not get close enough to help anyone else. He scrambled around the nose to the right side of the plane, but there the fire, whipped by the winter wind, seemed even worse.

Captain Marsh found the opening in the right side of the fuselage but could see no one about until he came on Andon, who also was looking for survivors. First Officer Dixwell, in pain with several fractured ribs, had gone off to look for a telephone. Marsh began to circle the burning plane, still searching for survivors, with Andon running behind him. They ran in a crouch, for the air was cooler close to the ground. The circle they made became wider and wider as the heat became more and more intense.

Then, suddenly, the emergency pistol flares, carried in the cockpit, exploded. They lighted the sky with brilliant color as Andon screamed at his pilot, "Hit the deck!"

Marsh fell to one knee, dazed. Andon threw himself to the ground. The flares sputtered out and the black of night, with snow still falling, returned. Captain Marsh resumed his quest, running around the plane until, exhausted, he told his flight engineer, "It's no use . . . It's too hot . . . too late to do anything."

Chapter
Eleven

NEWS of the disaster flashed to the nation with extraordinary speed born of chance.

While the larger New York International Airport at Idlewild was covered by the Associated Press, United Press and Reuters, only the AP assigned a reporter to La Guardia Field, and then only for eight hours a day. Tom Poster, the AP man at La Guardia, had got his "good night" from his city editor at 5:30 P.M., but Poster, a young man of effervescent curiosity, had stayed on at the airport to chat with a friend in the airport manager's office. Shortly after 6 P.M., he overheard the control tower radio calling for a police launch to hunt a missing plane. Poster went back to work. He phoned the control tower, learned that a Northeast plane was either missing or had suffered radio failure. He raced to the Northeast Airlines ticket counter where he confirmed the news. He phoned the first bulletin to his office within three minutes of the crash, then went after the details.

Samuel Leider, who had tried to get his daughter, Barbara Domash, and his two grandchildren off the plane during its de-icing delay, heard the first newscast about the crash on his car radio as he headed away from the airport on Grand Central Parkway. He left the parkway at the next exit and sped back to the airport. Robert Selmonsky, a Long Island lumberman and longshoreman, who also had tried to get his wife and child off the plane earlier, saw the flash of orange in the sky, turned his car about on Grand Central Parkway and headed back to the Northeast ticket counter. On the Manhattan Bridge, driving to Brooklyn, Joel Schwartz heard the news, thought of his father and fought his way through snowbound traffic back to La Guardia.

More than a hundred reporters and photographers of the city's newspapers, magazines and television stations hastened to the airport, to the prison's ferry slip in the Bronx, to Police Headquarters, to wherever news of an air crash could be gathered.

The whole complex of agencies and individuals who become involved in every plane crash was notified by one or another medium. Police Commissioner Stephen P. Kennedy was still in his office when the police ticker came through not long after 6 P.M. with the first report of a plane crash on Rikers Island. The commissioner, realizing that this was a catastrophe and one which might involve the prisoners on the island, decided to go to the scene himself. Deputy Chief Inspector Walter Klotzback, in charge of the Police Emergency Squad, headed a contingent that raced to the island to form a cordon around the wreckage, securing it for CAB investigators.

Commissioner Anna M. Kross, an energetic grandmother who headed the Correction Department, had just arrived home from her office when she called in to check on possible emergencies before releasing her driver. She hastened back to the car and directed her driver to rush her to the ferry slip.

Fire Commissioner Edward F. Cavanagh was being driven to Harlem to make a scheduled talk on winter fire prevention when his car radio picked up the alarm turned in from Rikers Island. As he rode along First Avenue near 110th Street, he radio-telephoned headquarters and was told that the fire involved a plane which had crashed on the island and had set fire to one or two houses and that there were survivors.

Commissioner Cavanagh instructed his driver to head for the 134th Street ferry slip in the Bronx, and, as his limousine sped along the snowy streets, he issued orders via his radio-telephone. He dispatched three fireboats to the scene; ordered two hook-and-ladder trucks and an engine to head for the ferry slip and try to find a means of reaching the island. He asked that available blankets in firehouses near the Bronx ferry slip be sent over. He telephoned Bellevue Hospital for disaster units and supplies of plasma, burn dressings and bandages.

The ferry slip at East 134th Street, one block from the huge Consolidated Edison powerhouse, soon became jammed with firemen, police, doctors, nurses, hospital attendants, and scores of newspaper reporters, photographers and television reporters, cameramen and their crews. Snow pelted the men, huddled in overcoats near the ferry slip. It was obvious that not all could board the ferry for the first trip to the island, and among newsmen, it was every man for himself. Repairs to the dock made it impossible for any vehicle to roll aboard the ferry. Commissioner Cavanagh was pleased that his department had had the foresight to send the pumper to the island before the dock work had begun.

On the island, it was some twenty minutes after the crash that the pumper, manned by Assistant Deputy War-

den Joehnk and an inmate, reached the scene. Behind it
came a truck carrying hose. The two trucks lumbered
toward the burning fuselage, then turned away toward
Farm Manager Hirschhorn's house, which had been set
ablaze by the flaming left wing.

Captain Marsh, seeing the fire engine, stamped his way
from his burning plane through the snow and slush to the
fire engine. While the island men struggled to set up the
pumping apparatus and the hose lines, Al Marsh screamed
at them to leave the burning house and tend to the burning plane. The men insisted their first responsibility was
the house, and Marsh, seeing what he thought was another
fire truck going by, jumped aboard. While he tried, perhaps incoherently, to direct these men to the plane, he was
taken to the main administration building.

Inside the building, Co-pilot Dixwell had telephoned the
Port of New York Authority office at La Guardia and
informed it that his flight had crashed on Rikers Island.
This was definite word, and at 6:22 P.M. the busy airport
resumed operations.

Eastern Airlines Flight 587, which had been waiting at
the head of the runway behind Marsh's plane, was cleared
for take-off. Captain George Bost revved the two engines
of his Martin 404, released his brakes, literally jumped his
plane over the chocks of snow which had built up beneath
his wheels, and roared down the runway. At 107 knots—
his V_2 speed—he lifted the plane into the air. The gear was
retracted. He left full power on in order to blow the remaining snow off his wings. The speed picked up to 130
knots, but as the plane began to climb, the BMEP and manifold pressure started to drop. Assuming that this was due
to carburetor icing, he called for carburetor heat. When
his co-pilot applied the heat, the indicator jumped to full

151]

cold on No. 2 engine. The engine feathered automatically. Then the power output on No. 1 dropped to about half. Airspeed fell to 105 knots—below V_2.

The twin-engine plane, then at about 250 feet, began to lose altitude. Captain Bost shouted to his co-pilot to unfeather No. 2. Cummings pulled the feathering button and the Martin 404 veered 35 degrees to the right as the No. 2 propeller began to windmill out of control.

The plane, veering toward the Whitestone Bridge, dipped to about one hundred feet above the East River. Then the No. 2 engine came to life with a surge of power. They began to climb again. Three seconds later, the left engine came back with full power. Shaken, Captain Bost took the plane up to 1,200 feet, sighed with relief, and then reoriented himself for the flight to Washington, D.C.

At the same time that the Eastern Airlines plane took off from La Guardia, Coast Guard Lt. Comdr. Brown left Floyd Bennett Field in a helicopter on his rescue mission. The craft had no windshield wipers and Brown and his co-pilot, Lt. Comdr. R. A. Lemmon, kept the side windows open so that they could wipe the snow from the windshield manually. They headed first for La Guardia. Flying at 150 feet, they had no trouble finding their way, despite the storm. They followed the parkways, which were lighted by the headlights of thousands of cars snarled in traffic jams.

At La Guardia, however, Brown flew to the boundary at the end of Runway 4 and there he was stymied. Beyond the boundary, it was pitch-black. He knew there were three Coast Guard buoys in the channel separating the airport from the island, but he could not see their lights. Since the helicopter was equipped only for visual flight, Brown did not dare to fly without some ground reference.

The airport suspended all take-offs and landings for fifteen minutes while Brown tried to find a way to cross the dark waters of Rikers Island Channel. Less than a mile from his objective, he was forced to give up. He landed at La Guardia and from the airport manager's office tried to reach someone on Rikers Island who could turn on some lights to guide him there.

He made several calls before he reached a prison guard. The guard told him that No, he could not leave his post to check on getting lights to help the helicopter. But the co-pilot of the crashed plane was there. Did he wish to speak with him?

Commander Brown talked with Dixwell for several minutes. He learned that the first party of doctors and nurses had arrived. But Dixwell did not know how to have searchlights turned on. Then Brown, his professional curiosity piqued, asked about the crash.

It was a hasty, disjointed conversation, but three questions stood out.

Had they lost two engines on the portside? Had they been flying on instruments or visually? What had been the first indication of trouble?

Dixwell, though he was in pain from the rib fractures, talked freely.

No, they had not had an engine failure. The first indication of trouble had been when he saw the ground coming up at him. He did not recall if they had been on instruments or visual; it was in that moment of transition.

Commander Brown understood the "moment of transition" to be that period when the pilot transfers his attention from visual references outside the cockpit to his instrument panel. For what it was worth, it was the first account of the crash given that evening.

The first ferryload of help, including Correction Commissioner Kross, Police Commissioner Kennedy and Fire Commissioner Cavanagh, arrived at the island at about 6:45 P.M. Firemen from three Bronx fire stations, unable to get their engine aboard the ferry, carried with them yards and yards of fire hose, hand fire-fighting equipment and blankets. The ferry was loaded to capacity with personnel from the three departments and from the first ambulances to reach the ferry slip, and with city officials. Despite a guard set up at the dock, some reporters had managed to sneak aboard.

Commissioner Kennedy established his headquarters in Dr. Farbman's small office in the administration building. The Police Missing Persons Bureau set up shop in an office nearby. The Police Aviation Bureau men went to the crash scene to await CAB investigators. When Commissioner Kross reached the wreckage, she asked in disbelief, "Is that all that is left?"

Against the background of snow, virtually all that remained of the plane was its white nose, the frame of its windshield and the tail, which, standing upright, still bore its white paint with its three double lines of blue and its identification number N 34954. Between the nose and the tail there was only the charred skeleton.

Before long, Commissioner Kross heard reports that some of the prisoners released for rescue work were escaping. Deputy Warden Harrison, thinking of his career, his family and the son he was supporting in college, ruefully admitted that he had heard the rumor, but there was no way to check it. Mrs. Kross, who brought a background of social work to her prison job, reassured Harrison. His decision to release prisoners for rescue work had been correct, she said, and she would support him whatever happened.

Commissioner Cavanagh, wearing his firefighter's rubber hip boots, took charge of the efforts to douse the burning wreckage. With great pride, he pointed at the water spouting from the hoses attached to the pumper. "Wasn't it lucky we got that engine over here?" he asked Commissioner Kross. "She sure is pumping!"

Meanwhile, others were arranging to transport survivors to the ferry and over to hospitals on the mainland. By that time, all the surviving passengers had been taken to the fourth floor of the prison's 200-bed hospital, where many of the inmates gave up their beds, or to the prison's large reception and visiting room on the first floor of the administration building.

The dreary, cavernous reception room, lined with benches, was a purgatorial scene. Some of the men and women were on their knees, saying prayers of thanks for their deliverance. Some sat on the benches, others stretched out on the floor. The number of survivors in the room grew from a score to twice that number, but there was no commingling. In their misery, they sought solace alone. Whimpers were heard more often than screams, though at first several women cried out: "Won't somebody do something?"

About twenty minutes after the first of the survivors had reached the room, Dr. Farbman arrived with a nurse, several inmate helpers and a large tray on wheels, bearing morphine, demerol, hypodermic needles, pans of vaseline, gauze pads and bandages. There was an initial rush by those who could walk. Then, when order had been restored, the room was effectively turned into a first-aid station. Dr. Farbman administered sedatives while his nurse and hospital orderlies went about the room dressing burns and wounds.

John Nolan, the college sophomore, permitted an inmate to apply vaseline to his burns but refused to sit or lie down. "As long as I'm on my feet, I'll be all right," he insisted.

Kenneth Kronen, who had caught the first blast of fire on his face and hands, paced the floor in a daze, waving his pained hands, heedless of his wife's pleas that he lie down. Mrs. Kronen tried to soothe little Richard, who, between sobs, complained that his ears hurt him. As she rocked her two-and-a-half-year-old son, whose face and ears had been burned, she worried about her other child, six-week-old Mark, whom her husband had given to a prisoner after their escape from the plane. She visualized the man putting her baby down in the snow to save an adult. Then, she was sure, her baby had frozen to death. She accepted the imaginary tragedy as fact, and she consoled herself that at least she and her husband still had one of their children. (Not until the following morning did she learn that Mark was safe.) When an inmate who had cared for her husband and Richard was about to spread vaseline on her grayish black face, Mrs. Kronen whispered, "How do I look?" The young prisoner gently answered, "You look fine, just fine."

The throbbing hands of Charles Naylor, the pianist, were treated in the reception room. Dry bandages were wrapped around Mrs. Naylor's burns because the supply of vaseline had run out. But even dry bandages helped ease the pain, shielding the tortured flesh from the air. The Naylors, like others in the room, took inventory of their burns and injuries, and Mrs. Naylor discovered that although her wool gabardine suit had protected most of her body, her nylon half-slip had disintegrated and utterly disappeared. Looking about the room, the Naylors realized for the first time that they had been relatively lucky. Many other survivors were in worse agony. Some, in shock, stared into space; others lay unconscious.

Nancy Tulowiecki sat on a chair, lost in the folds of a blanket. She refused offers of milk and spoke only occasionally. She brought tears to her father's eyes when she commented thoughtfully, "Dad, aren't we lucky the rest of the family didn't come with us, 'cause all of us couldn't have got out of that plane."

Her father, not seriously hurt, helped peel away the nylon stockings burnt into the skin of a woman sitting nearby. A solicitous prisoner offered Ed Tulowiecki a cigarette, but he declined, saying he smoked only cigars. "I'll get you one," said the prisoner, who ran to his cell block and got a cigar from a cellmate who was still locked up.

A Negro inmate, who must have been more than six feet tall and three hundred pounds in weight, walked slowly around the room, rocking a boy of about three in the cradle of his arms. He hummed softly and, oblivious to everything else in the room, never shifted the burden in his arms lest he disturb the child who was sleeping blissfully.

Captain Marsh found his way to the reception room after the prison truck, which he had boarded in the hope of returning to the burning wreckage, dropped him at the administration building. Entering the reception room, he was shocked: so many lay about in agony and he saw only one doctor and one nurse administering to them. He pitched in to help the nurse dissolve the sedatives, which were in pill form, so that they could be given hypodermically.

Cries of anger and protest from some survivors greeted him, but Norman Davis, who had wandered over from the mission house, told Marsh that he had seen the maneuver from the steep, almost perpendicular bank to the soft, flat crash landing. "It was a beautiful landing," exclaimed Davis. "How did you ever manage to level it off?"

Al Marsh, who no more knew how he had leveled off than he knew why the plane had crashed, mumbled something and moved on.

Later, the captain left the reception room in search of a telephone so he could inform Northeast's president of the crash. He got a call through to Boston and explained the situation to Hamilton Heard, then the airline treasurer.

Flight Engineer Andon, when he left the wreckage, found his way to the chicken house, where he came upon Emily Gately. He remained with her until she and others in the long, low building were transported to the island hospital.

Norman Davis also found his way to the hospital building and although he was not seriously hurt he was directed to the fourth floor where he was told to find a bed at the end of the ward. Walking through the long room, he was unnerved for the first time that evening by the moans and cries of his fellow survivors in the beds along the walls.

The first two beds on the right were occupied by Mason Benson and his wife. First, an attendant had helped the six-foot-four athlete to undress. Later, someone who seemed to be a doctor snipped off with surgical scissors the flesh that hung between his fingers, restoring shape to his hands. Then his hands and face were covered with vaseline and wrapped in gauze and bandages. His hands were so thickly bound that they looked as though they were encased in boxing gloves. Only Benson's eyes, nose and mouth remained uncovered. His wife was stripped of most of her clothing. Her wedding ring, which had become a vise on her swollen finger, and a gold bracelet, which had been burned deeply into her wrist, were snipped off and pinned to her underclothing. Both Bensons were given morphine and penicillin.

Farther down the ward, a nurse gave Emily Gately a shot of morphine and began to cut off her uniform. Disturbed because her new, still unpaid for suit was being ruined, Emily told the nurse, "I would have taken it off for you." The nurse only smiled. An inmate about twenty years old stayed beside the young stewardess, fetching water each time the terrible thirst returned to her scorched throat.

Then they brought in Dottie Steele, the senior stewardess. She was put in the next bed, but Emily, unable to turn her head, could not see her. She heard her friend's name mentioned by the doctor who was bandaging her and when the doctor moved on, Emily called to her.

"Is that you, Dottie?"

"Is that you, Emmy?"

"Yes."

"I saw Kay [Virchow] downstairs," Dottie Steele told her.

"Is the crew all right?"

"Yes."

"Thank God," said Emily.

Marilyn Lassell was brought in on a stretcher to a bed near those of the two stewardesses. Her young husband, remaining at her side, overheard a bit of the doctors' consultation at the foot of Miss Steele's bed. "She's got about five days to live . . ." he heard one doctor say.

At the rear of the ward, Norman Davis was told to undress, tie his shoes together at the foot of the bed and climb in. He did as he was told. But the sounds of people in pain and the odor of burned flesh made him uneasy, and he decided to leave the hospital. No one seemed to notice as he dressed. When he found he could not untie the knots in his shoelaces, he walked out of the ward unchallenged, carrying his shoes in his hand. He went down the staircase and out of the hospital building, not stopping to untie his shoes lest he be sent back, and headed toward the chaplain's house.

In the snow, his feet became frigid. So he paused beneath a streetlight, leaned against a pole and once again tried to unknot the shoelaces. In that position, looking perhaps like Elwood P. Dowd awaiting his mythical friend Harvey, Norman R. Davis was found by police and fire department officers. The circumstances took a tall order of explaining.

The island hummed with activity through the night. Everyone except inmates still locked in their cells pitched in. Scores of reporters and photographers tramped through the snow and slush. Often, their efforts to get the news conflicted with the rescue operation. There were some angry clashes. Survivors who were able to board the ferry were virtually mobbed by the press.

One veteran *New York Times* reporter, Edward Ranzal, rode about the island on the back of an open coal truck until he met an FBI agent whom he knew. He accompanied the agent around the island and while he himself never said he was from the FBI, he listened in on official conferences and acquired a wealth of inside information.

Another reporter tried to bluff his way into the prison hospital by posing as an official from the mayor's office. But Warden Silberglitt stopped him and, when he could not produce the proper credentials, he was escorted to the next ferry leaving the island. Others did get into the hospital and interviewed passengers; several also placed telephone calls to relatives of survivors.

At the Northeast Airlines ticket counter at La Guardia Airport, the shouts, accusations and wailing made such bedlam that one girl clerk broke down and wept along with those who had relatives and friends aboard the plane.

At the Northeast ticket counter in Miami, a first-aid station was established for those who waited long into the night to find out why Flight 823 was delayed. Handling the distraught relatives was Dorothy Richardson, who worked calmly and efficiently while worrying about the fate of her father, her mother and her younger sister. At 4 A.M., Northeast flew a special plane from Miami to New York for relatives and friends of those aboard Flight 823. Dorothy Richardson and Anne Marsh, wife of the pilot, were on this trip. Both were given sedatives.

By a half hour before midnight, all survivors had been taken from Rikers Island to hospitals in the Bronx and Manhattan. Long before that, pictures of the survivors appeared on television screens across the nation. One note of humor in all of the televised pathos was an interview with Mason Benson.

"Why were you going to Florida?" asked Walter Cronkite of the Columbia Broadcasting System.

"To get a burn," replied Benson, swathed in gauze.

A small band of firemen was assigned to remove the dead from the smoldering wreckage of Flight 823. They laid the bodies in three rows in the snow not far from the wreckage, and covered each with tarpaulin or blanket . . . Norman Chadwick . . . Lillian Nixon . . . Hyman Schwartz . . . Eileen Domash . . . The final count was twenty dead.

The prison inmates, when their work was done, filed back to their cells and were locked up for the night. Prison officials took their sixth and final count of the cell blocks shortly before 1 A.M. All were accounted for: not one prisoner had tried to escape.

Chapter Twelve

ONE of the first men to be notified that a plane had crashed on Rikers Island was Joseph O. Fluet, regional investigator-in-charge of the Bureau of Safety of the Civil Aeronautics Board. He had just skidded his way through snowbound traffic from his office at Idlewild to his home in Great Neck, Long Island. He was changing his clothes when his bedside telephone rang. It was 6:25 P.M.

Beside his phone was a list of telephone numbers of all airlines, local police units, search and rescue agencies and offices which might be concerned with an aircraft accident.

As a safety investigator assigned to the CAB's New York office, Joe Fluet was on call around the clock for any accident from Maine to Virginia involving a plane weighing over 12,500 pounds. An expert in his field, he had been called upon to help in difficult cases in Egypt, Great Britain and Europe. Since joining the CAB in 1942, he had dealt with more than one hundred accidents. At forty-nine years of age, he had spent thirty years in aviation and was one of the few men in aviation who held a pilot's license and a rating as an aircraft and engine mechanic.

Joe Fluet got the news from an agent of Northeast Airlines, who was fulfilling the requirement that an airline involved in an accident promptly notify the local office of the Bureau of Safety of the CAB.

Moving from his bedroom to his kitchen telephone, where he could jot down the information more comfortably, Fluet pumped his caller for as many details as were available. Fluet told the agent that all company records pertaining to the flight and to the plane must be held in safekeeping for the CAB investigation. He said he would be there in about an hour and asked the Northeast agent to request the police to have a launch ready to take him to Rikers Island from the airport's Marine Terminal.

Then Fluet called the control tower at La Guardia and learned that the weather had been above minimum, that the plane had been seen on radar proceeding straight out from Runway 4 and then making a sharp left turn toward Rikers Island. There was nothing known to be wrong with any of the ground navigational facilities at the airport. The plane had sent no word of trouble before the crash. . . .

He telephoned his two assistants, George Van Epps and Eugene Searle, and told them to meet him at the boat at Marine Terminal. He made several other calls, seeking as much information as he could gather before going to the scene. He called his automobile service station down the road and explained that he needed chains for his tires so that he could drive back to the airport. He had recently acquired a new government car and his requisition for snow tires had not come through. The garage man promised to put him at the head of the line of customers demanding chains. At 6:55 P.M., carefully noting the time, Joe Fluet left his house. At about the same time, Investigators Van Epps and Searle started out from their homes on Long

Island. And in the Washington headquarters of the CAB, James R. Durfee, the chairman of the five-man board, decided to ask board member G. Joseph Minetti, of New York, to take the case. A telephone call was put through to Minetti in Long Island Hospital.

Joe Minetti, a tall, swarthy man who sported a luxurious old-fashioned mustache, was on his customary weekend visit to his wife, who lay dying of a heart ailment. Minetti, not knowing whether she would survive this weekend, was torn between remaining with her and going to the scene of what was reported to be a major accident. "You go," his wife said, and Minetti went.

The Civil Aeronautics Board, established in 1938 and reorganized in 1940, is one of the smallest independent agencies in the federal government. Accident investigation and prevention is only one of its four functions.

It also regulates the economics of all commercial aviation in this country, certifying new air routes, approving rates and fares, and supervising all financial and business competition between the airlines. It assists the State Department in negotiating with foreign governments for the development of international air transportation. And, until the Federal Aviation Act of 1958, it prescribed the safety rules, regulations and standards for licensing pilots, flight engineers, stewardesses, mechanics and virtually everyone else having anything to do with the safety of airplanes, as well as certificating the production of airplanes, the operation of airlines, etc. This last important function was transferred to the newly created Federal Aviation Agency, which superseded the Civil Aeronautics Administration at the beginning of 1959.

For all of its duties and functions, the Civil Aeronautics Board has only about seven hundred personnel. By modern standards of government employment, this is austerity. In the investigating arm of the board, the Bureau of Safety, there are some one hundred and twenty employees, including secretaries and filing clerks. CAB investigators throughout the whole country number around sixty-five. The unofficial trademark of the investigator is the packed bag of clothes with toothbrush and shaving equipment. The men, earning civil service scale pay, are dedicated to a challenging job of accident investigation and accident prevention. At the first notice of a plane crash, four or five, sometimes more, rush to the scene. They work almost round-the-clock in the important first stages of gathering evidence. And, while these men are almost always successful in pinpointing the cause of an airplane accident, one lingering unsolved problem in most offices of the CAB is how to placate the wives of investigators who, after a while, resent their husbands' protracted absences.

The Civil Aeronautics Act of 1938 as amended gives the CAB the responsibility to investigate all accidents involving aircraft over 12,500 pounds and to report "the facts, conditions, and circumstances relating to each accident and *the probable cause thereof.*"

The words "probable cause" have always been open to semantic and subjective interpretation and as such have led to a great deal of the criticism of some CAB decisions on controversial accidents. But through the years the practical import of the words "probable cause" has come to mean: the logical conclusion of impartial experts who have studied all the evidence. It is analogous to a trial jury's verdict based upon the concept of "the preponderence of the evidence."

In almost any accident, witnesses rarely see the whole picture, and even more rarely are able to describe it objectively. The investigator, however, can piece together thousands of bits of evidence and information and, as an objective expert, can reach a conclusion as to the probable cause.

The CAB finds the probable cause in ninety-one per cent of the accidents it investigates. In the other nine per cent it states what evidence it has found and concludes that the accident's cause is undeterminable. Finding the probable cause leads the CAB to its corollary function of accident prevention. It recommends changes based upon its investigation, designed to prevent a recurrence of that "probable cause" of an accident. About half of its findings have led to specific alterations in airplane design, operating procedures, traffic control and other phases of air travel. And in the other half, where no specific change is recommended, the explanation of the probable cause has a salutary effect upon pilots, engineers, mechanics, dispatchers, controllers. . . . Pilots, whose own lives are involved, follow every detail of every accident and take heed when they learn the cause, or probable cause.

Joe Fluet, his mind working over the scant details he had obtained by telephone, drove doggedly through the snowstorm to La Guardia Airport. Where traffic was jammed to a standstill, he drove up the highway's embankment and around the stalled cars. Despite the weather, he made the trip from Great Neck to the airport, which normally would take thirty minutes, in a little more than an hour. He checked in briefly with Northeast Airlines to pick up the latest information and then hurried to the boat which would take him to the scene.

At the Marine Terminal, the police launch awaiting him was crowded with reporters, photographers, doctors, nurses and government officials. The launch captain, unable to clear the boat, insisted he would not set out with so much overload, and Fluet, with the help of others, sorted out those who could go from those who could not. Then the launch began moving through the murky channel which separated the airport from the prison island. It was still snowing.

Investigation of a plane crash is not unlike a police investigation of a homicide. The plane is the body, the distribution of wreckage is the room in which the crime was committed, and the flight crew, the passengers and ground observers of the accident are the witnesses. The suspect or suspects can be an engine, an electrical circuit, an instrument or any other part of the plane; or it could be the pilot, co-pilot, or engineer; and if sabotage is involved, it could be a passenger.

Arriving on Rikers Island, Joe Fluet's assistants, George Van Epps and Gene Searle, went off to view the body and the scene of the crime. Since the prison island was not readily accessible to the public, the wreckage had not been disturbed before the police emergency squad had roped off the area. Fluet, learning that the plane's crew had survived, went to the administration office to find them. Joe Fluet had known and liked Al Marsh for more than twenty years; both men had been barnstorming pilots in New England in the depression days of the 1930's. And, while this would not influence so experienced an investigator, Fluet could not help but think back to 1953 when Al Marsh had walked away from his wrecked plane and had telephoned him to come and investigate his accident at La Guardia field.

The investigator and the pilot came face to face again in a small room on the first floor of the administration building. They were not alone: the room swarmed with officials. Fluet asked Captain Marsh if he cared to talk to him now about the events leading up to the crash. Both men were aware that the crew had the right to ask for presence of counsel or of a union representative during any interrogation. Al Marsh said he and his crew would talk to the CAB officials, but preferred to do so in privacy. Various local officials insisted on hearing the story first-hand.

Fluet broke the impasse by prevailing on Captain Marsh to yield, and Marsh, Dixwell and Andon successively told their stories. Among those present in the small room were Fluet, Minetti, the district attorney of the Bronx, an assist-ant district attorney of Queens, Police Commissioner Ken-nedy and officers of the Police Aviation Bureau.

The most striking point in Captain Marsh's story was that he had been amazed that he had crashed on Rikers Island. He told his interrogators that he had had no idea that his plane had veered. He had thought he had crashed in the Bronx, straight ahead of Runway 4.

Marsh recited a chronology of Flight 823 as he knew it and the story he told under physical and emotional stress was substantially the same story he told through months of investigation and formal hearings of the Civil Aero-nautics Board.

There was some confusion about the exact number of passengers aboard, but the pilot said he could recall that the plane had not been overweight. It had been, he said, about 1,500 pounds under the authorized take-off maxi-mum of 97,250 pounds. Explaining the snow removal efforts, he assured the investigators that snow had not af-fected his flight. His take-off had been normal. In fact, he said, everything had seemed normal.

As he had seen his instruments, his plane had been

climbing straight away from Runway 4 on a northeasterly course when his co-pilot yelled, "Al, ground!"

Marsh gave the details on each instrument and insisted that no one and no combination of instruments had indicated that the plane was making a sharp left turn and flying down, not up and straight away, at 140 knots.

He had felt no sharp maneuver of the plane which would indicate that the trim tab on his rudder had been frozen. He had felt no bucking which would have indicated the plane was approaching a stall. He had felt no explosion which might have damaged any part of his plane. He had had no engine trouble.

Al Marsh insisted that he had been aware that in such weather his take-off was critical and he insisted that his full attention had been riveted to his instruments. Although no instrument had seemed to be malfunctioning, there must have been something wrong with at least one of them because, the pilot suggested, he had followed his instruments faithfully, yet had crashed.

To Joe Fluet, Al Marsh's story rang true. Marsh had answered every question. He had covered details from the time of his Miami-to-New York flight to the time he escaped from the burning plane. He appeared fully co-operative and eager to help. Yet, he could not explain how or why he had crashed.

This is not unusual. Seldom can a crew pinpoint the cause of an accident, and then only if there is a single, serious and obvious malfunction. But such malfunctions are rare in airliners which have multiple fail-safe systems and engines so powerful that the planes can remain aloft with two of four engines dead. Most often, a crash is caused by a series of small incidents and circumstances which build up to disaster.

The questioning of Al Marsh, Basil Dixwell and Angelo Andon at Rikers Island consumed some ninety minutes. The three men, interviewed separately, agreed that there had been no forewarning; no perception or instrument indication that the plane was turning and going down, no violent maneuver, no explosion, no malfunction. . . .

Joe Fluet walked away from the interrogation feeling that this accident most probably had been of an operational nature. From the crew's own story, it appeared that there had been nothing wrong with the plane. That left the area of human error. It meant that the investigators would have to delve into the thinking and actions of the pilot, the co-pilot and engineer—a far more difficult task than searching for the smallest malfunctioning item among the thousands of parts of a DC-6.

While the investigator-in-charge tended to put the emphasis on the crew's operations, he knew that every bit of the ill-fated DC-6A and every record and document pertaining to it would have to be gone over with scrupulous care. Aircraft accident investigators cannot afford to take anything for granted, must never jump to conclusions, and must not overlook the most innocent-looking detail, lest it be a clue.

Accident investigations proceed by a process of elimination, in the best tradition of crime detection. The investigators go over every single possible cause—the engines and its parts, the airframe and its parts, the instruments, the electrical circuits, the weather—and one by one they eliminate suspects until the culprit stands revealed.

In the investigation of this particular accident, the process of scrutiny and elimination would include instrument and electrical ground tests on a similar aircraft, instrument tests and studies at various manufacturing plants, combustion heater tests, de-icing fluid tests, analysis of burned deposits and materials from the plane, the wreckage distribution pattern, the tail section, the aircraft control systems, the engines and propellers, the attitude and speed of the plane on initial impact, the seating configuration, the loading of the plane, the de-icing, the maintenance, the flight planning and dispatch, the crew qualifications, statements by passengers, crew and ground witnesses, statements of crews who flew the plane prior to this flight, statements of crews who flew other planes in and out of La Guardia Airport before and after the fatal flight, statements of other airlines as to scheduled flights and cancellations, weather observations, control tower and radar observations, and special flight tests attempting to duplicate the flight path of the plane.

The inquiry into the thousands of factors involved in the crash would consume months of work and, after getting only an outline of what had happened from the statements of the crew, Joe Fluet began to plan the organization of his investigation.

After the interrogation of the crew, he filled in Minetti with as much information as he had gathered from other sources and they discussed the next steps. CAB policy called for one of the Board's five members to be assigned to a major accident and it was apparent that Minetti, a New Yorker, would be the man.

The two men braved an onslaught of reporters as they left the administration building to inspect the plane wreckage. They were faced with a recurring problem: How much information, if any, should they make public? CAB policy forbids disclosure of investigation data until the board has issued its final report: prematurely published information can be misleading and prejudicial. But to refuse all information leaves the field open to those who would prejudge, often mistakenly. Fluet and Minetti told the reporters very little.

The investigators made a preliminary inspection of what was left of the plane and, as best they could with limited lighting, they tried to trace the pattern of wreckage. More detailed work was left for daylight, but it was important to reconstruct, if possible, the entire flight path from Runway 4 to Rikers Island. The men stayed until 2 A.M., then returned to the airport control tower where they worked through the night.

A meeting to organize the full-scale investigation convened at 10 o'clock that Saturday morning in a control tower room crowded with more than fifty men, representatives of the airline and of the manufacturers of the airplane, the engines, the propellers, and the instruments; of the Air Line Pilots Association, the Flight Engineers Association; and of law enforcement agencies, including the police, the district attorneys' offices and the FBI.

Fluet, as man in charge, outlined the investigation. Reviewing what had been learned so far, he said, "Something abnormal happened aboard that plane, and it is up to us to find that abnormality and to find it objectively and not by prejudging."

The investigation was divided into five separate areas, each headed by a CAB representative: operations and witnesses, structures, powerplants and propellers, instruments and electrical systems, and aircraft airworthiness and maintenance.

Interested parties joined the group or groups of their particular interest, at their own expense. The Air Line Pilots Association, whch maintains an air-safety and engineering division consisting of some three hundred and fifty regular airline pilots, assigned a union member to each of the five task forces. The union paid each pilot's salary while he was away from his flying job. Northeast Airlines likewise assigned a man to each of the five groups. Manufacturers of the instruments aboard that particular DC-6A put one of their men on the instrument group.

The CAB, although relatively small and impecunious, is able to conduct thorough and costly investigations because of the enlightened self-interest of the aviation industry. Everyone in the industry has a stake in safety. Hence everyone is interested in finding the cause of an accident and preventing a recurrence. Everyone also has a reputation to protect, a reputation which involves dollars and cents. The plane manufacturer, the man who makes the engines, the man who makes the instruments, or the radios, or the propellers—each has his product to sell, and in aviation, the product must be proven good and safe. The pilots and the flight engineers have a personal as well as professional standing to maintain. The airline equally must guard its reputation. Thus, the self-interest of the interested parties works to the benefit of the CAB and of the public, with each investigating group, composed of experts checking and counterchecking one another, ferreting out facts which lead to a conclusion of the *probable cause* of the accident. At the head of each group is a CAB investigator motivated by no special interest other than his own integrity and his pride in his ability to discover the truth. Heading the whole investigation, co-ordinating the efforts and results of the five groups, is the investigator-in-charge, who in this inquiry was Joe Fluet.

The "suspects" were singled out quickly. Investigator Van Epps, heading the operations and witnesses group, reconstructed the take-off of Flight 823. The radar observations from the control tower indicated the plane left the ground somewhere between halfway and two-thirds of the way down the runway, a normal take-off. The plane flew straight about twenty seconds beyond the end of the runway, then went into a bank and turn to the left. It veered an incredible 119 degrees off course and crashed about twelve seconds later.

Rikers Island itself was scoured by air and on the ground for clues as to how the plane had hit. This was one of the most important phases of the investigation, for it would tell what had happened to the plane just before it crashed. A wide distribution of wreckage might indicate an explosion in the air, due possibly to sabotage, fire or a faulty part. A single big crater would indicate a nose dive.

Joe Fluet accompanied the men of the structures group in a survey of the island from a police helicopter. Criss-crossing the scene, they could see where the plane had chopped through the tops of a group of small trees. They could see where the plane hit the ground and they could see the series of propeller slashes along the ground indicating the plane's flat slide.

On the ground, the investigators searched for and found every bit of metal, cloth or smudge which came off the plane. They worked in a half-mile area like detectives dusting for fingerprints. Five surveyors were put to measuring precisely the location of each item ripped from the plane. They found and measured two hundred separate items and marked each piece on a huge map. Each item was photographed as it was found before it was carted away for more intensive scrutiny. Some even were put under a microscope. Then the marks that the plane made on the trees and ground were measured and photographed.

From these markings, the surveyors computed the precise path of Flight 823 when it crashed. The plane came down, they found, at an angle of descent of seven degrees, which was a fairly steep dive of about 1,700 feet per minute. The evidence also showed that the plane hit the trees with its left wing banked some nineteen degrees. It broke off branches at an average height of almost fifteen feet above the ground. Its first ground contact was made by No. 1 propeller, the left outboard, which sliced through the earth. Then the left wing tip hit, then No. 2 propeller, then the aft end of the fuselage, then No. 3 propeller and then No. 4.

The preliminary evidence pointed to the first suspect: that the pilot somehow lost control and the plane, an unleashed tiger, flew itself into the ground before the pilot could analyze by his instruments what was happening. The problem with this theory was to determine why the pilot lost control of the plane. Had something gone wrong with the plane? Or wrong with the pilot?

After surveying the distribution of the wreckage, the investigators began examining the remains of the plane. This was the autopsy. As painstakingly as a doctor dissects the body of a homicide victim, when the cause of death is unknown, the investigators went over the corpse of the plane. Their search eliminated one suspect and brought to light two others.

The investigators were able to disprove the assertions of some passengers that one or both of the left engines had caught fire in flight. The engines were found to have broken off the wing before the plane ignited; they were recovered intact, and neither showed signs of internal fire before or after the crash.

In going over the tail section, which had not been destroyed by fire, the investigators found evidence in the left stabilizer (the left horizontal wing of the tail) of an internal explosion. This could jibe with the statements of two stewardesses and several passengers that they had heard an explosion in the tail about the time the plane hit the ground. The investigators found that the skin had been blown outward, indicating the source of the explosion was inside the stabilizer. However, they also found long scratches on the stabilizer's bottom skin, indicating it had skidded along the ground before it broke open. Which came first, the explosion or the ground slide? The entire stabilizer, including a duct that carried heat to that part of the tail, was sent to the New York City Police Department laboratory for minute examination.

The investigators also found a suspicious, black tarlike substance in the plane's two pitot tubes, which, protruding from the underside of the plane, measure the air flow past the plane and hence the craft's airspeed. The tubes were sent to the FBI laboratory in Washington for analysis.

With great care, the investigators removed each of the flight instruments from the burned cockpit. Fire-blackened, they had suffered varying degrees of damage, but they yielded a good deal of information. The face of one cockpit clock showed the shadow of the minute hand, which had stopped at seven minutes after the hour. This indicated that fire had not consumed the cockpit and its instruments until five minutes after the crash.

All the instruments were packed in separate boxes and taken to the CAB offices in the Federal Building at Idlewild Airport. There, the men carefully recorded every reading they could get from the smudged, charred gauges. Then they sent them off to their manufacturers for analysis and testing. Were the instruments working and accurate before the crash? Or could they have misled a pilot into catastrophe?

And so it went. The wreckaged airplane was dissected, and its engines, generators, heating system, radio equipment and other parts were sent to the manufacturers for analysis.

There were other suspects, too. How much snow had been on the wings at take-off? Could ice have formed to destroy the airflow over the wings? Could ice or snow have frozen the trim tabs on the rudder? If so, a sudden release of the trim tabs could have produced a violent turn. Was the plane overweight?

Chapter Thirteen

THE answers to the outstanding questions were not easy to find. In fact, the tragedy of Flight 823 confronted the Civil Aeronautics Board with one of the most difficult cases it ever encountered. The facts of the flight itself were simple and known. The crew had survived to tell their story. The wreckage yielded up most of the craft's components. Everything was there to be studied. Yet, the *why* of the crash did not readily reveal itself.

In many cases, the *probable cause* appears almost at once. When John Gilbert Graham, a twenty-three-year-old youth, bought $37,500 in vending machine insurance policies on his mother's life and placed a homemade bomb in her suitcase before she boarded a DC-6B in Denver on November 1, 1955, CAB investigators were able to pinpoint the exact location of the bomb in the wreckage. A bomb exploding inside a plane shatters the fuselage into pieces much smaller than pieces torn from the plane in the crash itself. The investigators found the telltale fragments, plus the obvious remains of the bomb, centered in what had been the aft baggage compartment, where only two suitcases had been lodged. The rest was easy. The trail led to Graham and the FBI made the arrest two weeks after the crash.

Sabotage, while difficult to prevent, is easy to solve. When a National Airlines DC-7, bound from New York to Miami, crashed near Wilmington, North Carolina, on January 6, 1960, the investigators were stymied until they found the body of passenger Julian Frank, a young attorney from Westport, Connecticut, some sixteen miles away from the main wreckage of the plane. In his remains, they found foreign particles, which under analysis turned out to be parts of a homemade bomb. Frank had insured his life for almost one million dollars. Although the CAB found the probable cause of the crash to be the explosion of dynamite and a dry-cell battery in the vicinity of Frank, it left it to the FBI, the police and the courts to determine whether Frank or someone else had placed the bomb aboard the plane.

The most feared misadventure, the mid-air collision, also is relatively easy to solve because of the radar and radio networks that survey the skies. Even when planes collide in a remote area, unseen by radar, and no one survives, CAB investigators can reconstruct what happened from the physical evidence. Such was the case when the Trans World Airlines Super-Constellation and United Airlines DC-7 collided at 21,000 feet and crashed into the Grand Canyon in Arizona on June 30, 1956. Investigators sifted thousands of pieces of wreckage in the Grand Canyon and hauled out the pieces which provided clues to the collision. Then bit by bit the fragments were labeled and fitted together. A minute inspection of the reconstructed plane sections showed patches of paint from one on the other. This evidence, coupled with flight plans, routes and other data, enabled the investigators to show

how the airliners converged and why the pilots had not seen each other. The tragedy demonstrated the need for better air traffic control from the ground.

No matter how difficult or easy an investigation, the procedures follow the same pattern. In the six weeks following the Rikers Island crash, while the physical evidence was being analyzed in laboratories stretched halfway across the country, investigators worked in other areas.

The weather picture of February 1, 1957, was reviewed. From pilots who had flown in and out of La Guardia that afternoon and evening, the investigators learned that not one had encountered any difficulty with snow or icing in flight. From witnesses in the control tower and in the Eastern plane waiting to take off behind Flight 823, it was learned that the take-off appeared normal; that it became airborne where expected and flew straight out from Runway 4. The ground crew helped to review every aspect of the snow-removal operation. A special committee scrutinized the plane's maintenance history from the day it was manufactured to the day it crashed. At first, the investigators thought there might have been more than the usual number of pilot squawks concerning instrument failures. But on review and reflection, they could find no pattern of failures that would bear on the crash. Each pilot complaint dating back to the Flying Tigers' use of the plane had been corrected and signed off by a mechanic.

Then the reports from the laboratories came back. The engines, propellers, generators and the heating system got clean bills of health, particularly the heater in the tail where an explosion had been suspected. "The empennage heater control assembly was still operative within Surface Combustion Corporation inspection tolerances even though it had been damaged by impact. There was nothing noted on any of the equipment which indicated other than normal operation," said the engineering department of the Surface Combustion Corporation, which had manufactured the heaters.

The FBI reported that the material found in the two pitot tubes were small pieces of charred wood and bark. The CAB investigators concluded that the wood and bark had entered the tubes during the plane's slide and had burned along with the plane. They could not have affected the operation of the tubes before the crash.

The Police Department laboratory reported finding pine needles and pieces of pine tree branches inside the left horizontal tail stabilizer. It suggested that the pine needles indicated that the explosion had ripped open the stabilizer before the plane made contact with the pine trees. But in a supplemental report the laboratory clarified its earlier opinion. Noting that the scratch marks on the under surface of the stabilizer were continuous across the torn skin, the laboratory concluded: "The airplane was probably sliding at the time of the explosion. The skin of the stabilizer was not torn off but the opening enabled this exploded area to collect the piece of pine tree branch and the pine tree needles after they were broken free by the forward parts of the airplane."

The Douglas Aircraft Company reported that the rudder trim tab and its control system, recovered almost intact from the wreckage of the plane, had been tested and found to be within proper operating standards. To further test the theory that the trim tab might have been frozen by ice and its sudden release might have caused the sharp left turn, the investigators decided to simulate a jammed rudder trim tab on a similar plane.

On March 23, the investigators made five different flight

tests, in a DC-6B supplied by Northeast, to test the trim tab theory and to try to duplicate the path of Flight 823.

George Steers, Northeast's assistant operations manager of the airline, flew the plane. Clark Willard, chief pilot of the airline, occupied the right-hand seat as co-pilot. George Van Epps sat between and behind the two pilots in the flight engineer's seat, while Joe Fluet sat in a jump seat and Richard Miller, another CAB investigator, watched from the companionway.

Flying at 6,000 feet for safety's sake, the rudder trim tab was set several degrees to the left but the co-pilot held the plane on a straight course by applying right rudder with his foot pedal, all without the knowledge of the pilot. Then, suddenly, the co-pilot released the rudder pedal. The rudder deflected suddenly to produce a sharp left turn. But the aircraft banked and turned only fifteen degrees before the pilot easily corrected for the turn within five seconds. This turn was minor compared to the 119-degree turn of the DC-6A, tending to eliminate the frozen trim tab theory.

Motion pictures taken of the instrument panel of the test flight plane showed that three different instruments—the turn-and-bank indicator, the artificial horizon and the C-2 compass—clearly indicated the nature of the turn in time for a pilot to take corrective action.

The investigators were not as successful in their attempt to duplicate the flight path of the crash. Simulating Flight 823 as closely as possible as to weight and operations, they took off from Runway 4 and, shortly after becoming airborne and while still over the runway, began a co-ordinated turn to the left. Speed was controlled at 140 knots. Gear and flaps were taken up. The plane banked to forty-five degrees before it passed over the point where the DC-6A had crashed. While they succeeded in reaching the spot of first impact and the final resting spot of Flight 823, the test plane had begun its turn while still over the runway. Flight 823, however, had been observed, partly from the ground and then by radar, to have flown straight out past the end of the runway before turning.

On their second test, the investigators started out by flying two hundred feet above Runway 4, proceeding past the end of the runway but not yet abeam of Rikers Island. Again they made a co-ordinated steep left turn, banking forty-five degrees. This time they missed the first point of impact of the crashed plane by some one hundred and fifty feet to the left, but they passed over the final resting place of the wreckage.

On their third test, they repeated the beginning of the last test but they did not start the turn until they were abeam of Rikers Island. This time, they banked the test plane fifty degrees, but they missed the first point of impact by about three hundred feet and passed to the right of the wreckage.

In attempting to reconstruct the actual flight path, the investigators could proceed by deduction and logic. They knew the plane had taken off normally from Runway 4, had proceeded past the end of the runway, had veered left in a co-ordinated turn that had not been felt by pilots or passengers, and had descended until it crashed. They knew also that Al Marsh, following Northeast operating procedures, had lifted his landing gear as soon as his plane was airborne, had retracted flaps when it was about two hundred and fifty feet up, and had called for his first reduction in power when the plane was between two hundred and fifty and three hundred and fifty feet above the ground.

They knew that when a pilot retracts his wing flaps, his plane loses some of its lift, its rate of climb subsides and the plane levels off. But as it levels off, it picks up speed and as the speed increases, the plane resumes its steady climb to cruising altitude. The essential ingredient of this aerodynamic formula is that speed must be maintained to keep the plane flying.

What apparently happened to Flight 823 was that when Captain Marsh retracted his flaps at 125 knots, his heavily weighted plane did not have sufficient speed to maintain level flight and began to lose altitude. Captain Marsh's reduction of power would have tended to worsen the situation: he was getting less power just when he needed more.

In mushing toward the ground, the plane's nose would have remained up, in a climbing attitude, while the plane actually was sinking. Then the plane would have lost its ability to fly. It would have stalled and fallen off, to the right or to the left. It therefore was possible that Flight 823 had veered in a steep bank, which could not be duplicated under controlled conditions in a test plane, and yet been in a turn so co-ordinated that it was not felt by those inside the airliner.

While a plane approaching stalling position usually will buck against the wind, sometimes it does not. An airplane does not stall as an automobile does. Its engines can be roaring at maximum power and the plane still may stall, either because of its attitude in the air (its bank too steep, its nose too high) or because its weight is too great for its speed.

While this might explain how Flight 823 had crashed, it would not explain why Al Marsh had not seen what was happening on his flight instruments and taken simple corrective action. Either the instruments had failed, or Captain Marsh had failed to see and interpret correctly what they showed.

The instruments had been suspect from the first on the basis of Captain Marsh's own account that none had indicated the turn and descent. Many things could have caused one or more instruments to go wrong, a short circuit in one or several, or a power failure to all. Except for the altimeter and the airspeed indicator, all instruments in every DC-6 are powered by electricity. But, to guard against a major short circuit, the DC-6 has three separate sources of electric power. The pilot's instruments are powered from one source, the co-pilot's from another. A third source is available at a flick of a switch in the event a warning flag pops up to indicate a short circuit.

Since the electrical system had been utterly destroyed in the fire, the investigators relied on statements of the crew and passengers and on logic to evaluate the possibility of total electrical failure. Noting that the recovered generators had been within operating specifications, the investigators ascertained that the cabin lights, the FASTEN SEAT BELTS and NO SMOKING signs, the cockpit lights and the landing lights had all functioned normally. This left little doubt that the basic electrical system had been working.

All of the powerplant gauges had been destroyed in the fire, but some of the flight instruments were recovered relatively intact.

The investigators could learn little from the two ADF's or two gyro compasses because their heading gyros had tumbled after the impact of the crash. But the two Collins course indicators, one on each pilot's instrument panel, were slaved to the two separate compass systems, and were so designed that their azimuth rings, which provided the compass directional information, would remain at rest if electrical power were removed. Their readings could not be moved or changed by vibration or shaking. The first officer's course indicator showed a heading of 282 degrees and the captain's showed 272 degrees. Significantly, they reflected the heading of the plane when it hit the ground and came to a final rest, indicating the plane's compass system had indeed been functioning properly.

The investigators conducted numerous tests in a similar DC-6 to determine what would happen to an artificial horizon indicator, a turn-and-bank indicator, and the gyro compasses if their electrical power were cut off. Each instrument continued to function for two or three minutes before tumbling out of synchronization—indicating that if they had functioned properly on the ground, they must have continued to operate normally in the less than one-minute flight.

With the instruments checked out, the investigators turned with new emphasis to the flight's operational aspects. A vital consideration, aside from the actual handling of the plane by the pilot, was weight.

The weight and balance information on Flight 823 had disclosed that something was amiss. The manifest had been destroyed in the fire and the duplicate copy had been erased and corrected by Northeast after the crash to account for the extra baggage and change in passengers. It was some seven weeks after the accident that George Van Epps decided to recheck every item on the load manifest. Earlier, he had found the simple errors involving the baggage and passengers.

But in rechecking the empty operating weight of the plane, Van Epps tracked down an error of more than two thousand pounds. It was a simple mistake. On December 31, the day before the DC-6A was delivered, the Flying

Tiger Line telegraphed to Northeast the empty operating weight as 61,527 pounds. This was the empty operating weight as used by the Flying Tigers under the regulations governing cargo planes. It did not include the weight of the three-man crew (figured at 170 pounds each), the two stewardesses (at 130 pounds each), the crew's luggage (75 pounds), the stewardesses' kits (24 pounds), the ADI fluid (291 pounds), the 120 gallons of oil (900 pounds) and the sandwich service (32 pounds). These items, amounting to 2,092 pounds, would not be included in the empty operating weight of a cargo plane, under civil air regulations. They would be added to the plane's empty weight for each flight.

But, under the regulations for passenger airliners, they would be included in the empty operating weight. So, Northeast had been operating the DC-6A since January 9 with 2,092 pounds that it had not figured.

The investigation then turned to whether Northeast had weighed the plane before putting it into service. The answer was "No." It had accepted the Flying Tigers' figure. Had any CAA inspector, in certifying Northeast for the Florida route, checked to determine whether the plane had been weighed? The answer was "No."

With the extra 2,092 pounds, the plane's gross weight on take-off was recalculated by the investigators at 98,575 pounds. This was 1,325 pounds over the maximum gross weight of 97,250 pounds authorized for Flight 823, as given to Captain Marsh.

But, as George Van Epps and others reaudited the actual weight, they also recomputed the authorized maximum weight. Considering temperatures and wind, and allowing for the runway gradient, they came up with a figure of 98,840. This put the actual take-off weight at 265 pounds under the legal maximum: Flight 823 had not been over-loaded.

Two months after the accident, the fact-gathering phase of the investigation was completed. Laboratory reports and the results of tests were in, and statements from everyone connected with any phase of Flight 823 had been collected. The time had arrived for a public hearing of the evidence.

On April 2, in a ballroom of New York's Belmont Plaza Hotel, the hearing began. The room was jammed with interested parties and the press. Now all the facts gathered on an off-the-record basis would be put on the record. In effect, members of the various CAB investigation groups would present their evidence, and the airline, the pilots, the flight engineer and manufacturers would have the right to cross-examine and the right to contest any evidence or opinion presented.

At the head of the room, sitting as a panel of the CAB board of inquiry, were board member Minetti and five members of the CAB's Bureau of Safety: Robert W. Chrisp, chief of the Hearings and Reports Division in Washington; Leon H. Tanguay, acting associate director of the bureau in Washington; Joe Fluet, investigator-in-charge of the New York office; John E. Pahl, acting chief of the Technical Division in Washington; and William S. MacNamara, operations specialist from Washington.

Although the hearing had every appearance of a trial, it was essentially part of the fact-finding procedure to determine the probable cause of the accident and to prevent similar accidents in the future. The difference between the hearing and a trial was important. No witness had the right to refuse to testify. There were no formal pleadings or issues. There were no recognized adverse parties. No one could object to discussion of any subject allowed by the hearing officer. The sole purpose of the hearing was to get at the facts and to get those facts on the record. To protect witnesses, no part of the hearing could be used as such in a civil suit for damages. The final accident investigation report of the CAB could not be introduced in a civil trial. And, no CAB investigator could testify as an expert witness. The idea, simply, was to free the fact-finding inquiry from involvement in any legal battle over monetary damages.

Captain Marsh testified at great length. He spent hours explaining his one-minute flight. He reviewed his use of each instrument in his cockpit. Undoubtedly some of the experts in the hearing room were surprised to learn that he had relied on his rate-of-climb indicator rather than his altimeter to determine his probable altitude. While an altimeter is not precisely accurate immediately after take-off, the rate-of-climb indicator is even less precise because of its inherent time lag. It could show a climb a second or two after the plane had begun to descend.

Listeners also were surprised to hear Captain Marsh relate that he had relied on his ADF as his primary directional instrument rather than on his artificial horizon or turn-and-bank indicator. The ADF, a low-frequency instrument, is a rough, not a precise, indicator of direction. Most pilots use the artificial horizon on take-off to ascertain that the plane is straight and level with the horizon and therefore heading straight away. The turn-and-bank is used as a double check on the artificial horizon.

Nevertheless, any one of these instruments should have informed Captain Marsh of so steep a bank as would have had to be involved in a 119-degree turn—not to mention a descent when the plane should have been climbing.

First Officer Dixwell admitted that he had stopped monitoring his instruments for several seconds to watch Flight Engineer Andon reduce the power setting of the plane. And Andon told in detail of his preflight preparation and his observations during flight.

Fifty-six witnesses testified. Control tower men, weather forecasters, CAB field investigators, Northeast ground crews, dispatchers, loading agents, and eight passengers were among those heard. More than 1,200 pages of testimony were recorded. Hundreds of documents and records were introduced as exhibits.

When all the witnesses had been heard, Captain Marsh and Dixwell were recalled and questioned again on minute details of the flight. On April 11, nine days after it had begun, the hearing ended. It had been one of the longest in CAB history.

The investigation now moved into another phase. All documents and testimony were transferred to the CAB offices in Washington. Copies were distributed to the five sections of the Bureau of Safety: Operations, Engineering, Analysis, Investigation, and Hearings and Reports. Each section prepared preliminary reports on its phase of the investigation.

Now the men of the Bureau of Safety had to come to a decision, if possible, based on the evidence at hand. Expert analysis was involved. The subject was complex and experts differed. They hammered out their differences in long, sometimes heated discussions.

The separate reports then went to the Hearings and Reports Division, where writers prepared a preliminary written report to be submitted to the five CAB members for adoption. Again, discussions were long and arduous. The field investigators from New York conferred with the operations and engineering experts in Washington. The evidence was reviewed again and again.

Finally, many months later, the preliminary report was submitted to the CAB members. The debate was renewed over how to word the final report, how to shade the nuances and fairly assess the blame for the *probable cause* of the accident.

On March 6, 1958, more than thirteen months after the crash, the Civil Aeronautics Board adopted its accident investigation report. Four days later, it was released to the public.

THE final report reviewed in detail the facts and circumstances of Flight 823. It explained how each instrument had been examined, tested and absolved of malfunction. Then it presented its reasoning in determining the probable cause of the accident, which took twenty lives.

The CAB report can best speak for itself:

> In analyzing the operational phase of this flight, a careful study was made of all known facts in conjunction with the testimony of the crew. In the analysis it must be borne in mind that the aircraft was airborne approximately thirty-one seconds during which time it traveled a distance of some 6,600 feet and turned approximately 119 degrees to the left.
>
> Both Captain Marsh and First Officer Dixwell testified that the take-off was normal and that they observed no indication of any irregularity or deviation from the take-off heading. Testimony of the crew and passengers appears to be in general agreement in that the aircraft was not banked when it passed over the runway and there was no feeling of any abrupt changes in attitude during the flight. One passenger, with 400 hours of piloting experience [Norman Davis], testi-

Chapter Fourteen

fied that the aircraft was in a steep left bank just prior to the time he observed a leveling action of the aircraft immediately prior to impact. Considering this testimony, the time consumed in reaching the end of the runway, and the time involved in attempted recovery, it must follow that the turn, although steep, was a co-ordinated one and was accomplished within a period of some 20 seconds. Thus, the rate of turn was in the magnitude of six degrees per second.

From the testimony, it is evident that the aircraft's acceleration after take-off was normal and that Captain Marsh followed the prescribed company procedures in ordering the landing gear to be retracted, the wing flaps raised, and power reduced to METO. Considering the short time involved in the execution of these commands, it is considered highly probable that, when the power was being reduced to METO, the wing flaps were still either in the process of retracting or were just completing the retraction. During this period, in which the configuration of the aircraft was progressively changing to en route climb, it would be imperative that the pilot devote his full attention to his flight instruments in order to control the aircraft effectively.

Captain Marsh testified that he observed the flight engineer in the process of reducing to METO power. Without reference to the proper flight instruments at this time, Captain Marsh would be unable to take the proper control action. Captain Marsh stated that his prime concern was the airspeed, rate of climb, and direction. Further testimony indicated that he used his ADF indicator as a primary directional instrument, took little advantage of the C-2A Gyrosyn compass or azimuth card of the course indicator, and made little reference, if any, to the artificial horizon or turn-and-bank indicator. He did not use the magnetic compass.

Captain Marsh testified that he knew at the time that the C-2A Gyrosyn compass had been somewhat unreliable. This fact, and the knowledge that the course indicator was a repeater, should have alerted the captain to check the C-2A Gyrosyn compass against the magnetic compass at the engine run-up position. Following take-off he also disregarded the altimeter and substituted the rate-of-climb indicator, referring to the altimeter only on every third or fifth scan of the panel, attaching little importance to this instrument. From this testimony it is evident that Captain Marsh did not take advantage of his full instrumentation nor did he rely upon primary instruments.

A consideration that cannot be overlooked is the possibility of the pilot becoming disoriented by reason of attempting to remain visual for too long a period after take-off and losing visual contact before the transition to instrument flight. However, Captain Marsh was very emphatic in his testimony that he went on instruments when the gear was retracted and did not look out again until he saw the ground immediately prior to striking it. Snowfall occurring during the take-off at night, with the landing lights on, could have produced a glaring effect or a period of temporary blindness, and the time involved after reference to the instruments may not have been sufficient to allow return to normal vision. This consideration cannot be completely ruled out; however, because of Captain Marsh's testimony, it would appear not to have been a major contributing factor.

Both pilots stated that they went on instruments shortly after take-off. They described their duties and manner in which they performed such duties. Both stated everything was normal. Neither pilot was able to give a reasonable explanation for the unusual attitude of the aircraft.

The possibility of pilot fatigue was considered. The crew reported on duty some ten hours prior to the accident. Total flight time involved a period of approximately four hours. A delayed departure and waiting for the aircraft, which was fully loaded with passengers for several hours, to be released for flight may have caused the crew some concern; however, there was no evidence to indi-

cate that fatigue was a factor in this accident. Had the
flight to Miami been completed in the planned time, the
total duty hours of the crew would not have exceeded
their contract limits.

It is customary for the first officer to monitor the flight
instruments during an instrument climb-out. According
to his testimony, First Officer Dixwell monitored the
engine instruments and the flight instruments until the
command was given for METO power. He then devoted
his attention to monitoring the flight engineer's actions
without further reference to the flight instruments. This
action, according to his testimony, consumed quite a few
seconds and lasted until his attention was attracted to
the outside immediately prior to striking the ground. Had
First Officer Dixwell had opportunity to devote his attention to the flight instruments during this critical period
in the flight he would undoubtedly have detected the
deviation from course.

The cockpit of N 34954 was equipped with both electrical and pitot static flight instruments. With the exception of the C-2A Gyrosyn compass and one cross-pointer
indicator, the instrumentation was identical on the pilot's
and co-pilot's panels. Captain Marsh testified that, with
the exception of a turn from 40 toward 45 degrees, no
turns were made during the flight and that no indication
of a turn or bank was displayed on any of the flight instruments. Both pilots testified that there was no warning
of any instrument failure. Assuming that there had been
a failure of a directional instrument and that the indicator
either remained in a fixed position or assumed a rota-
tional motion, the perceptibility of a turn not evident in
that instrument would be evident on other instruments
as would a turn to follow a rotating directional indication. Similarly, a failure of an attitude instrument and
any attempt to follow an erroneous reading would be
revealed by other attitude and directional instruments.

There is no evidence that any such irregularities did
occur and there appears to be no reason why the radical

departure from course would not be displayed on the instrument panel. Based on this and other facts of record, the Board can only conclude that Captain Marsh either did not properly observe his flight instruments or failed to refer to the proper instruments in his control of the flight.

In conclusion, the Board has conducted an intensive study of the evidence accumulated in this investigation in an effort to arrive at a reasonable solution of the facts. It has been shown beyond a reasonable doubt that the aircraft and its accessories were functioning normally throughout the short flight. This being so, we must conclude with reasonable certainty that the events leading up to this accident point to the actions of the captain, who was at the controls and in complete command, in that he did not demonstrate the skill and care required of an airline pilot in the performance of his duties. The captain's contention that he thought everything was normal until the first officer sighted the ground and quickly advised him, further substantiates the Board's opinion that the captain did not have control of the aircraft.

The CAB then presented its formal findings and determination of the probable cause:

On the basis of all available evidence the Board finds that:

1. The aircraft, crew and carrier were currently certificated.

2. The gross take-off weight of the aircraft was under the maximum allowable and properly distributed.

3. The weather at the time of take-off was above the prescribed company minimums.

4. The aircraft, immediately following take-off, made a left turn of approximately 119 degrees and a descent.

5. The pilot and flight crew did not observe or interpret any instrument indication of a left turn or descent.

6. The heading indications of both fire-seized course

indicators corresponded closely to the impact heading of the aircraft.

7. These instruments had been functioning properly until the time of impact.

8. There was no failure or malfunction of the power-plants.

9. There was no airframe failure or control malfunction.

10. There was no electrical power failure or malfunction of instruments prior to ground impact.

11. There was no fire prior to ground impact.

12. As a result of fuselage deformation, the main cabin door jammed, hindering evacuation of passengers.

13. The main cabin lighting system became inoperative during deceleration and the emergency inertia lights did not actuate.

<u>Probable Cause</u>

The Board determines that the probable cause of the accident was the failure of the captain to (1) properly observe and interpret his flight instruments and (2) maintain control of his aircraft.

The Air Line Pilots Association vigorously protested the CAB findings, charging that the Board was blaming the pilot because it could find no other reason for the crash. The union contended that it was possible for the compass system of the plane to have led the pilot astray and to have left no trace of malfunctioning. The union, seeking a reason other than pilot error, has kept open its own investigation on the chance that some future crash might explain the Rikers Island accident. Should ALPA come up with new evidence, it can present it to the CAB and reopen the Board's investigation. The CAB never closes a case, knowing that in aviation the future might shed light on the past.

The tragedy of Flight 823 has remained controversial among pilots. Many find it difficult to understand how a veteran pilot could have failed to see a 119-degree turn on his instruments during a critical take-off.

One theory popular with pilots varies only in degree from that of the CAB. This holds that the plane mushed because of its weight and inadequate speed, but on a straight, on-course heading from Runway 4. Because of drift due to the northeasterly wind, Dixwell yelled, "Al, ground!" when the plane was losing altitude but still on course. Then, when Captain Marsh looked up from his instruments, the plane fell off to the left and dived to the ground. This theory would better explain how a pilot might miss the indications of his instruments.

The theory, however, fails to take into account the estimate, based on radar observations from the control tower, that the 119-degree turn took at least twelve seconds. This would mean that twelve seconds elapsed between the time Dixwell saw the ground and the crash. It does not coincide with the testimony of Captain Marsh and Dixwell that the plane struck the ground within a few seconds of the co-pilot's warning. Twelve seconds would have provided ample time for Marsh to avert disaster—or at least to try to avert it.

Most of the arguments revolve about the probable cause of the probable cause. In other words, what made Captain Marsh lose control? What minor or major incidents led up to the final cause?

Taking into consideration the natural desire to provide service as soon as possible, one may question the wisdom of Northeast Airlines in inaugurating its Florida service with the minimum training of pilots. One may question the efficiency of the Civil Aeronautics Administration in permitting the airline to start its operation so soon. One may question the airline's policy of having a captain, with fewer than one hundred hours' experience in a new and different plane, flying with a former chief pilot instead of a regular co-pilot, who would have been monitoring instruments instead of double-checking on the flight engineer. Such a co-pilot might have seen the beginning of the turn and dive in time to avert the accident. While this does not relieve the pilot-in-command of full responsibility, a co-pilot is in the cockpit precisely so that he can help monitor instruments during critical take-offs and landings.

One can question Captain Marsh's judgment in taking off in marginal weather. It was officially above the allowable minimums, but he might have taken into account his lack of experience in a DC-6, which handles far differently from the lighter twin-engine planes he had been accustomed to flying.

Next to the handling of the plane, the load was probably the most vital factor in the accident. While the CAB computed the total weight at 265 pounds under the allowable maximum, it gave Northeast the benefit of every technicality. However, the allowable maximum weight for every plane on take-off always is calculated conservatively and a plane usually can be flown safely at several hundred pounds above that figure. But Al Marsh might never have flown that plane that night had he known that the margin was only 265 pounds. That kind of margin is scant indeed when factors such as immeasurable snow on the wings are present. And, had Captain Marsh taken the plane up that night with the knowledge that its weight was so close to the maximum, he might have flown it differently. He might have been alert to the danger of mushing. He might have kept his flaps down and his engines at full power until he had climbed to 500 feet and gained more speed.

The pity of it is that Captain Marsh was following his airline's standard operating procedures for a take-off in a DC-6. He was flying conservatively, by the book, as he had on all other take-offs in that plane. But this time, apparently because of its full load, the plane lost its lift, its ability to fly. And Captain Marsh failed to see what was happening in time to control his plane.

In the luxury of Monday morning quarterbacking, you can point the finger at many people, practices and agencies:

One might wish Captain Marsh could have known the correct weight of the plane. One might also wish the CAA inspectors had checked to make sure the plane had been weighed. And, looking back, one might wish the Commerce Department and Congress had not slashed requested CAA appropriations in the early 1950's, thus depriving the agency of adequate funds to check and supervise such operations as those of Northeast Airlines. One might also wish there could be special weather minimums for snowstorms.

Captain Marsh, in following his company's standard operating procedures, was not following the procedures of other airlines. Captain Marsh raised his flaps and reduced power at the points prescribed in his company's manual. However, most airlines flying the DC-6A or DC-6B prescribe that flaps not be retracted before reaching a minimum altitude of 500 feet.

This minimum is intended to provide time, space and speed to recover if a plane begins to settle after flaps are retracted. At 500 feet, a DC-6 will have developed a speed of about 140 knots, rather than 125, before flap retraction.

After the Rikers Island accident, Northeast adopted the 500-foot rule.

AFTERMATH

Chapter Fifteen

CAPTAIN Alva V. R. Marsh never piloted an airliner again. He allowed his airline transport license to lapse simply by not taking his next required semiannual physical examination. Since the tragedy, his hair has turned grayish-white, and his friends say the bounce has gone out of his step. To a few close friends he has sometimes wondered aloud why he, who had devoted his entire working life to flying, had been singled out for three crashes.

Captain Marsh is still in aviation. Northeast created a new desk job for him, in which he assists the airline's operations manager in the scheduling of pilots and planes and in other administrative details.

Basil Dixwell has returned to flying status with the airline and has qualified as captain-in-command of DC-6s. Angelo Andon continues as a flight engineer.

The three stewardesses, who were among the most severely burned, have not returned to their jobs. Each spent several painful months in hospitals, then went home to recuperate sufficiently to undergo plastic surgery, which, three years after the accident, is still being continued.

Of the seventy-five passengers who

escaped alive, twenty-five were severely burned. The worst-maimed passenger was Mrs. Chopelas, who survived primarily by dint of will power. Her lungs poisoned by smoke, she was unable to speak for two weeks. Her eyes seared by fire, she was blind for three weeks. Fire had consumed parts of her ten fingers and charred her face, her hands, arms, legs and upper back. She spent almost four months in two hospitals. In three years she has undergone forty-five major operations. Her doctor and hospital bills totaled more than $50,000. She has resumed a more or less normal life, but has given up going out in public. In an out-of-court settlement of her suit against Northeast, she received $257,000.

Mrs. Chopelas' settlement was the largest by far; the lowest went to the nonrevenue passengers, whose passes had contained a waiver of the right to sue. Most of these received little, if any, more than their medical bills.

All of the passenger damage suits were settled out of court by 1959, two years after the accident. Most airline accident suits drag on for several years and are settled only after one or two test cases have been tried in the courts.

Out-of-court settlements in aviation cases are based on the degree of negligence, the severity of injuries and the amount of damage suffered. The passenger must prove a prima-facie case of negligence on the part of the airline or airplane manufacturer before a judge will allow the case to go to a jury.

In most negligence cases, damage awards are far higher for personal injuries than for death. Juries seem to be more sympathetic toward a person maimed than toward a widow and children.

But there is another factor: under common law, until 1846, death extinguished the right to sue, and a widow got nothing. When state legislatures did establish the right to sue for the death of a relative, they limited the amount recoverable—a thoughtful precaution for the protection of railroads. These limitations have been whittled away over the last hundred years, but thirteen states still maintain them. In Massachusetts, for instance, the maximum is $20,000.

Even worse, the maximum anyone can recover from an airline for personal injury or death resulting from an international flight is $8,300. This limit was set in 1929 by the Warsaw Convention, an agreement of western European nations to which the United States subscribed in 1934. Its purpose was to permit airlines to obtain insurance at reasonable rates in the early days of aviation when one crash might have bankrupt a company. Revision of the Warsaw Convention is under consideration by the Senate Foreign Relations Committee. Bar associations advocate that the United States abrogate this archaic agreement, leaving unlimited the amount of collectible damages. The airline industry is urging a compromise, raising the maximum to $16,600.

Air-crash litigation has become so complicated and so technical that only the specialist usually is qualified to handle a case that goes to trial. When a victim of an air crash instructs his family attorney or a general practitioner to sue, the attorney usually retains a negligence trial lawyer, who in turn usually retains an aviation law specialist.

In this manner, most of the suits in the Rikers Island accident which had not been settled immediately were referred to Stuart M. Speiser of New York, whose firm handles most of the airline crash cases in the United States that go to trial. Speiser, pilot of a B-24 in World War II and holder of a commercial pilot's license with four-engine rating, started practicing his specialty after the war. His firm, in which seven former fliers are members, is virtually the only one equipped to handle the technical research and investigation required in a passenger's aviation negligence suit. When his firm's investigation, which often parallels that of the CAB, is completed, either the original negligence trial specialist takes over for the trial or Speiser's own firm handles the trial as well.

In the Rikers Island case, Speiser's firm took depositions from the crew of Flight 823, from the ground crew involved in snow removal and loading, and from the management officials of the company.

Going over the same ground as did the CAB investigators, the lawyers sought not only the probable cause of the accident, but evidence of negligence. An airline, like a railroad, bus or ship, is a "common carrier for hire" and must provide each passenger with the "utmost care" in getting him to his destination. If anything less than that "utmost care" can be shown to have resulted in injuries, passengers can collect.

When the taking of pre-trial testimony from employees of Northeast was completed in 1959, the Northeast insurers decided to settle.

Settlements were based upon hard calculations. A man who must give up a $25,000-a-year job will receive far more than a man who must forgo his $5,000-a-year job because of identical injuries. A man who obviously will have medical expenses for the rest of his life will receive more than his widow would have received had he been killed. The settlement for the death of a man is greater than that for his wife because the loss of his earning capacity can be measured in money—and it is only money that the insurance companies can pay. The widow of a thirty-five-year-old executive will get more than the widow of a fifty-five-year-old executive who was earning the same salary, because the younger man was deprived of twenty more years of earning power. Of course, other factors too enter into settlements—not the least of them being the lawyer's ability to bargain.

For their efforts following the crash, fifty-seven inmates of Rikers Island penitentiary received immediate releases or reductions in sentences. New York's Mayor Robert F. Wagner awarded the Department of Correction Medal of Honor to Deputy Warden Harrison and gave recognition to forty-three other prison employees, including the chaplains, doctors and nurses.

The troubles of Northeast Airlines, which had not had a passenger fatality in its first twenty-three years of operation, did not end with the Rikers Island crash. Seven months later, on the foggy night of September 15, a Northeast DC-3, making an instrument landing approach to the New Bedford, Mass., airport, fell short of the runway into a swamp. The two pilots and ten of the twenty-one passengers were killed. The CAB attributed the crash to pilot error. Its investigation showed the pilot had abandoned his instrument approach in an attempt to make the approach visually. Eleven months later, on another foggy New England night, a Northeast Convair 240, making an instrument approach to the Nantucket, Mass., airport, crashed about 1,500 feet short of the runway. Again both pilots were killed, along with the stewardess and twenty-two of the thirty-one passengers. The CAB bluntly declared the probable cause was "the deficient judgment and technique of the pilot" in failing to abandon his landing approach when a visibility of one-eighth mile, which was below legal landing minimums, was reported. Like the pilot in the New Bedford crash, he had descended dangerously low while still a considerable distance from the runway.

Ten days after the Nantucket accident, the CAA launched a special, full-scale investigation into the operations of Northeast Airlines. The agency took inspectors from other tasks and assigned them to help the Boston CAA office, which was staffed with four operations inspectors, two maintenance inspectors and one electronics expert. The investigation scrutinized the airline's manuals, procedures and practices, but the emphasis was on the competence of the line's 125 pilots. They were subjected to instrument-proficiency flight checks with a CAA inspector in the cockpit, and were restricted to visual (or clear weather) flying until they proved their abilities.

The inspectors, several of them from Washington, worked full time at this investigation from August 25 to October 7. They found deficiencies in operations and they discovered also that many of the deficiencies had been known and tolerated by the Boston office CAA inspectors.

The investigators reported that Northeast maintained an inadequate pilot-training program, largely because it had barely enough pilots and planes to cover its schedules. The airline's records of pilot training were so skimpy, the investigators found, that it was impossible to determine the qualifications of the flight crews. Check pilots, the CAA discovered, were not familiar with their duties and were not carrying out the prescribed flight checks. Company manuals prescribed a periodic ground school training and familiarization program for pilots, but the airline was not carrying it out.

Operations decisions, which should have been carefully planned in advance, were being made on a daily basis. The investigators found inadequate liaison between pilots and the maintenance department. The operations and maintenance departments were not given sufficient authority to make day-by-day decisions, the investigation revealed. Almost all such decisions had to be approved by one man, the president of the airline, George Gardner.

The airline and the CAA set out to correct the deficiencies. Northeast shifted its top management; George Gardner became chairman of the board of directors and Alfred A. Lane, vice-president in charge of operations, was returned to his old status as a pilot. James Austin, vice-president for traffic and sales of Capital Airlines, was appointed president and general manager of Northeast, and brought with him his own staff of top management.

Despite Northeast's efforts to win customers for the New York–Miami route, the line failed to show a profit for the years following the award of the "Golden Route." In mid-1960, the board of directors of Northeast voted to merge with Trans World Airlines. Such consolidation requires CAB approval.

The trend in the jet age of the 1960's appears to be toward airline mergers and consolidations. With jets costing $5,000,000 each, the carriers must seek economies, and combining complementary seasonal schedules of different lines is economical. A merger with Northeast would give TWA, which flies cross-continent and overseas, the lucrative New York–Miami route. It would mean the eclipse of Northeast as an entity and would extend TWA's service not only from New York to Miami and points between, but to New England and parts of Canada.

The proposed merger, still under study by the CAB,

is opposed by Northeast's two competitors on the New York–Miami route—National and Eastern—on the grounds that it would make TWA too powerful a rival on the Golden Route and might spell financial collapse for National and Eastern.

Several years back, Eastern absorbed Colonial Airlines and extended its own route structure into New England and Canada. National has proposed a merger with Pan American Airways, but the CAB disapproved on the ground that Pan American had been favored in awards of international routes in the 1930's and 1940's on the assumption that it would have no domestic routes. In vetoing the proposal, the CAB ordered Pan American to sell the stock it had been acquiring in National. However, a Northeast-TWA merger is expected to have a far better chance of CAB approval.

Another proposed combination expecting CAB approval is that of Capital and United Airlines. Capital, plagued by unprofitable short hauls between New York and Chicago, petitioned the CAB in 1960 for approval of consolidation with United Airlines on the ground that it faced bankruptcy because it could not pay installments due on its purchase of turbojet British Viscounts. United is one of the country's most financially stable airlines with well-established long-haul routes, primarily between New York and San Francisco and Los Angeles.

The two most important events in aviation since the Rikers Island accident, although not in any way connected with it, were the advent of the jet airliner and the establishment of the Federal Aviation Agency. Fortunately, they occurred at approximately the same time.

The Boeing 707 and the DC-8 in 1959 and the Convair

880 in 1960 revolutionized air travel, as did the DC-6 and Lockheed Constellation after World War II. The jets, cruising at 600 miles per hour, doubled the speed of their immediate predecessors and almost doubled the passenger-carrying capacity. A single jet airliner costs about three times as much as the latest piston plane, but its earning capacity is three to four times as much. Its relatively vibration-free comfort makes it doubly attractive to the public, and its safety record as a new plane has been phenomenal. The jet engine is so much simpler and more reliable than the best of the piston engines that its rate of failure is far less than that of piston planes. The pure jet has proved itself so rapidly that it appears likely that the 300-mile-an-hour DC-6s and 7s and the Constellations and super-Constellations may soon be relegated to carrying cargo.

The only danger appears to be a financial one: that present-day jets may be made obsolete in a few years by larger and better ones, traveling at speeds up to two thousand miles an hour. The airliner able to go from New York to San Francisco or London in two hours or less is already on the drawing boards. But would it be economically feasible at this time? No, say most aviation experts. They advise that production of the super-jet be put off for at least ten years, until today's expensive jet craft have served their time and paid their way. Instead, most of the aviation industry is looking forward to the production of small jets, with a capacity of fifty to eighty passengers, which could be used for cities with airports too small to accommodate the DC-8, Boeing 707 or Convair 880.

With the advent of the jet age came establishment of the Federal Aviation Agency on January 1, 1959. The need to remodel the government's supervision of aviation became clear following Congressional investigation of the factors behind the collision of two airliners over the Grand Canyon in June, 1956.

Public attention was drawn to this tragic mishap which took 128 lives. There also was an increasing number of other mid-air collisions, particularly between commercial airliners and military planes. Among the hidden flaws in aviation safety revealed by the Congressional investigation was that military and civilian planes using the same air space were under different controls: little more than luck was preventing other collisions. President Eisenhower appointed former Air Force Lieutenant General E. R. Quesada to head an Airways Modernization Board to recommend the streamlining of air traffic control over the United States.

The Federal Aviation Act of 1958 was the result. General Quesada was appointed head of the new Federal Aviation Agency. The FAA absorbed the Civil Aeronautics Administration, taking over from it air-traffic control and the administration and daily supervision of safety regulations governing pilots, flight crews, maintenance and the general operations of commercial airlines, as well as of private planes and pilots. It tightened up control over military aircraft when they operate in civil airways. It took over from the CAB the promulgation of regulations and standards for flight and maintenance safety of all commercial and private aviation. It took over the air traffic control functions of the Airways Modernization Board. And, most important, it was given adequate funds, for which the old CAA had been pleading for years. In 1956, for instance, the CAA had a budget of $162,000,000 and 18,000 employees. In 1960, the FAA had a budget of $690,000,000 and 42,000 employees.

The new Aviation Act vested in one man, the Federal Aviation Administrator, enormous powers to regulate and supervise all airline activities which touched on public safety. General Quesada, a determined, forceful administrator who served as FAA head until January, 1961, did not hesitate to use his power. He began enforcing every safety regulation on the books, revising inadequate regulations and establishing new ones. But the major part of his program was enforcement.

The CAA, lacking money to hire the number of inspectors it needed or to train adequately those it had, was obliged to let the aviation industry police itself. It relied on the premise that everyone in the industry had a self-enlightened interest in safe flying. For lack of flight inspectors, the CAA had designated company pilots to serve as check pilots for the required semiannual proficiency flights of their fellow pilots. For lack of rating examiners, the CAA chose outstanding company check pilots to serve as flight examiners of pilots qualifying on new equipment. The CAA inspectors had time only to make spot checks, flying and testing pilots at random and infrequently. Thus, the pilot group became dominant in deciding the everyday problems of safety in many but not all airlines. Government regulation was carried on in a country club atmosphere of co-operation, good will and self-policing.

With the almost concurrent advent of jets and the FAA, General Quesada ruled that all pilots qualifying to fly jet airliners would have to pass flight proficiency rating tests by FAA inspectors. The FAA began eliminating the use of pilots designated as rating examiners. While the old CAA could not get the money from Congress to acquire its own four-engine piston planes to train its examiners and inspectors, the FAA in two years has acquired more than one hundred planes, including four commercial jet airliners and a ground simulator. It also has been able to send its inspectors to military installations for training on the Air Force counterparts of the commercial jets. Inspectors also are being sent to the manufacturers for indoctrination on the innards of the new jets. The FAA idea has been to train its inspectors to the point that, while they might not be so expert as the airline pilot, they would be able to judge whether or not the pilot was able to control the plane within the rigid specifications established by the FAA.

The FAA still does not have enough money to maintain a staff of inspectors large enough to give the regular six-month proficiency checks to all pilots, but it has increased the number of spot checks. In an attempt to make the maximum use of its inspectors, the FAA has initiated a program of specializing inspectors. Rather than assign a certain number of inspectors to all operations of an individual airline, the FAA has been experimenting with assigning a number of flight inspectors to, say, all Boeing 707s, and having them make flight inspections of those planes used by all airlines in one area.

The FAA has revamped the semiannual medical examination of pilots. It has decreed a compulsory retirement age of sixty for all pilots, on the ground that a man over sixty has slower reflexes and is more liable to a heart attack than a younger pilot. It has strengthened cockpit procedures, including the enforcement of an old regulation prohibiting pilots from leaving the cockpit in flight to socialize with passengers.

It has reinstituted a regulation that every airline must maintain and conduct recurring ground school training to refamiliarize pilots and flight crews with emergency procedures. The FAA in effect has been raising the minimums of safety practices. This has affected some airlines, but not all, for many airlines have long maintained standards higher than the government minimums.

The FAA has moved into other equally important areas of safety. It has launched a multimillion-dollar program for better air traffic control, better radar surveillance, better airport facilities. It has expanded its Oklahoma City Aeronautical Center for the training of FAA pilots, mechanics and inspectors. It has opened its own research center in Atlantic City, where it can experiment with and test new equipment.

The FAA efforts are only part of the activity designed to bring about complete safety in the air. The airlines, the pilots union, the manufacturers of planes and parts, private aviation research foundations—all are working toward that goal, and statistics prove they are making gains.

Yet the risk always will remain in flying. Despite statistics and safeguards, every flight is an individual, complex undertaking—as a study of the Rikers Island accident shows—and there is potential risk in every flight. But there is a risk in every means of transportation—even walking.

Aviation as we know it today is a new industry, perhaps just about reaching maturity. On the day Pearl Harbor was attacked, the airlines of this country were operating approximately 360 commercial passenger planes, small twin-engine craft which cruised at about 140 miles per hour. Half of this civilian air fleet was turned over to the Army Air Force when the United States went to war. Civilian air travel within the United States was cut to the bone.

After the war, from about 1946 to 1950, the airline industry went through a period of transition, acquiring equipment and pilots while striving to catch up with public demand for air travel. In reality then, the aviation industry and air travel as we know it today can be said to be only ten years old. In those ten years, it has made giant strides in speed, capacity, routes, comfort, and, above all, safety.

But there are gaps. Giant strides remain to be taken. No doubt they will be. Travel by air is the way of the present and the way of the future.

Advice to the Passenger

There are certain questions almost every air traveler would like to ask a pilot or anyone connected with aviation. These questions the author has posed to many of the aviation people he met while researching material for this book. The advice given below is a composite of the answers he received. It does not reflect the opinions of any one expert. It should, at best, serve as a guide, for there is no final, absolute answer to total safety in the air.

1. *Which airline should I take to go from —— to ——?*

This is perhaps the most frequent question put to the expert, and there is no answer to it. One can say Airline A is better than Airline B because it invests more money in pilot training, higher standards of flight operations and in maintenance. But no one can foretell that any one flight of Airline A is safer than one of Airline B. The safety record of all major airlines is so good that statistics on past accidents give no clue to the likelihood of the next.

2. *Is it safer to fly by day than at night?*

Not really. Except for the actual landing and take-off, virtually all airline flying is done by instruments within the cockpit and since pilots have greater confidence in their instruments than in what they can see beyond the cockpit, day and night flights are equally safe.

3. *Is it safer to fly in clear weather than in storms?*

Obviously, yes. But the margin of added safety is so slight that only the most cautious will avoid flying in rain or snow storms. Modern airliners are designed to withstand turbulence. Yet, a passenger does have the right to judge the suitability of the weather against his need to travel. The Government sets minimum weather standards for flying, but an airline, a pilot and even a passenger has the right to choose not to fly in particularly bad weather.

4. *Should I abandon a flight if the plane is delayed at the airport by mechanical trouble?*

Usually, no. A passenger should be thankful for the delay, knowing that the malfunction is being corrected before take-off. Every pilot loves his own life dearly and will not endanger it by trying to fly a defective plane. Yet a passenger should know that he has the right to quit a plane and have his fare refunded before take-off.

5. *Where is the safest location to sit on a plane?*

In the tail section. Again, the margin of added safety is small, but it is the forward section of the plane which usually bears the brunt of a crash. In several notable accidents, the only survivors were among those seated in the rear of the cabin. It is wise also to sit near an exit, or at least to note the location of the nearest exit and to read the printed instructions on how to open an emergency door or window.

6. *Does a seat belt really add to one's personal safety in a crash?*

Definitely. A securely fastened seat belt is the best single safety factor in the control of the passenger. Not only will it help him bear the impact of a crash, but a seat belt should be kept fastened throughout a flight as protection against the possibility of being jolted out of one's seat by unexpected air turbulence or a sudden maneuver of the plane.

7. *Is there any protection against a person carrying a bomb aboard a plane?*

No absolute safeguard has yet been devised. Baggage is inspected where there is any reason to suspect sabotage. But the few instances of bombers do not warrant a time-consuming search of every piece of luggage and every person who boards a plane.

217]

However, each passenger can avoid inadvertently carrying a fire hazard aboard by taking care not to pack matches, lighter fluid or other combustibles in his luggage.

8. *Is any one type of clothing better to wear than another?*

Yes. There is an added measure of safety in wearing woolen clothing as protection against fire. Synthetic fabrics are highly inflammable.

Is It Safe To Fly?

The answer to the question, "Is it safe to fly?" will be seen best from a perusal of the CAB statistics on the following pages.

Over the years, it can be seen, more and more people are traveling by air, more miles and more hours are spent aloft in the nation's airliners. At the same time, since 1952, the passenger fatality rate has been maintained at less than one person per 100 million passenger-miles flown.

It can also be seen that there is no pattern over the years or in any one year to the type of accident most likely to occur next. Accidents resulting from a faulty aeronautic design were considered a thing of the past until the crashes of the Lockheed Electra in 1960. The multimillion-dollar radar network guarding the skies over metropolitan New York was the nation's showcase of effective air-traffic control, and two modern airliners belonging to two of the biggest and most safety-conscious airlines collided and crashed over New York City on December 16, 1960.

The year of the Rikers Island accident, 1957, happened to be the best year of airline safety, and yet a perusal of the accidents of that year will show a variety which defies pigeonholing. The accidents for 1957 show only those of the scheduled U.S. passenger planes. Space does not allow a review of the safety record of private, corporation or cargo planes. Yet, it should be pointed out that of all phases of flying, including military and private planes, airline travel is by far the safest.

The increase in the safety of airline flying over the years can be seen in the gradual decrease in life insurance rates for airline pilots to a point in 1955 when airline flying was no longer considered a hazardous occupation. The following rates of extra premiums for airline pilots are those of the Equitable Life Assurance Society of the United States.

Period	Annual Extra Premium per $1,000 Insurance
1917-1940	$25
1940-1941	15
1941-1945	10
1945	5
1945-1954	3
1954-1955	2.50
1955-present	0.00

Scheduled Passenger Service, U.S. Domestic Operations

Time of Accident	Date	Location	Airline	Aircraft	Aircraft Damage	Fire	Total Aboard	Division of Injury Crew			Passengers		
								F	S	M/N	F	S	M/N
0001 CST	1/6/57	Tulsa, Oklahoma	American	CV-240	Destroyed	None	10	0	3	0	1	3	3

The weather was rapidly deteriorating as flight was making an instrument approach which was continued below the company's approved minimums. The aircraft collided with the ground approximately three and one-half miles from the runway.

Time of Accident	Date	Location	Airline	Aircraft	Aircraft Damage	Fire	Total Aboard	Crew			Passengers		
								F	S	M/N	F	S	M/N
1207 EST	1/16/57	Pittsburgh, Pa.	Capital	DC-3	Substantial	None	23	0	0	3	0	0	20
			TWA	L-749	Substantial		43	0	0	5	0	0	38

As the aircraft approached the intersection of two taxiways, the DC-3 crew observed the Lockheed to the right. Braking was ineffective due to ice on the strip and the aircraft collided as the DC-3 turned left.

Time of Accident	Date	Location	Airline	Aircraft	Aircraft Damage	Fire	Total Aboard	Crew			Passengers		
								F	S	M/N	F	S	M/N
2031 CST	1/16/57	Louisville, Kentucky	TWA	L-749	Substantial	None	46	0	0	6	0	0	40

The gear was extended for landing but the crew was unable to get a "down-and-locked indication" on the left gear. The approach was discontinued and several emergency gear extensions were made in an unsuccessful attempt to get a green light on the left gear. When the gear appeared fully extended a landing was made. The aircraft was almost stopped when this gear retracted.

| 2315 EST 1/25/57 Fort Eustis, Virginia | National | CV-340 | Substantial | None | 42 | 0 | 0 | 3 | 0 | 0 | 39 |

On an IFR flight plan, the flight had received several vectors from radar control to the Newport News ILS outer marker. However, as it established visual contact and observed a lighted runway to the left, the flight plan was cancelled and an approach made. As touchdown was made, the pilot realized he had landed at the wrong airport. The aircraft could not be brought to a stop on the short, slippery runway and it ran off the end, stopping at the base of a 15-foot embankment in soft, muddy ground.

| 1802 EST 2/1/57 Rikers Island, N. Y. | Northeast | DC-6A | Destroyed | After Impact | 101 | 0 | 0 | 6 | 20 | 25 | 50 |

The aircraft made a left, descending turn of approximately 119 degrees immediately after takeoff into instrument weather conditions. The captain believed the flight normal until the copilot called out his observation of the ground an instant before impact. The aircraft struck the ground in a descending, slightly left wing low attitude, skidded for approximately 1,500 feet and burned.

Time of Accident	Date	Location	Airline	Aircraft	Aircraft Damage	Fire	Total Aboard	Crew			Passengers		
								F	S	M/N	F	S	M/N
Scheduled Passenger Service (Cont'd)													
0402 CST	2/7/57	Jackson, Miss.	Delta	L-049	Substantial	None	39	0	0	5	0	0	34

During an ILS approach to the airport at Shreveport, La., the captain took over control from the copilot and started a missed-approach procedure, but not in sufficient time to prevent the aircraft from colliding with the ground. A pull-up was made but the left gear could not be retracted. The flight returned to its take-off point at Jackson and landed. During the landing roll the gear retracted.

| 1530 CST | 2/8/57 | Louisville, Ky. | Eastern | L-1049 | None | None | 28 | 0 | 0 | 5 | 0 | 1 | 22 |

The flight encountered sudden, unexpected severe turbulence. The cabin attendant and several passengers were injured as a result of being thrown about in their seats.

1127 CST   3/5/57   Nr. Memphis,   American   DC-7   Substantial   None   46 | 0 0 5 | 0 0 41
Tenn.

While cruising at 14,000 feet, No. 1 engine and propeller over-speed. A climb was entered in an attempt to quickly reduce air-speed and shortly thereafter the propeller broke free, striking the aircraft cabin and causing explosive decompression. An im-mediate descent was initiated and a landing made at Memphis without further incident.

1138 CST   3/10/57   Louisville,   Eastern   M-404   Destroyed   After   34 | 0 0 3 | 0 1 30
Ky.   Impact

The copilot was making the approach and turned into final high and close, in relation to the approach end of the runway. At an altitude of 1000-1500 feet above the runway, the captain took over control, nosed the aircraft down sharply, and continued a steep, power-off approach. As power was not applied the flareout was ineffective because of the low airspeed, resulting in an exces-sively high rate of sink at instant of touchdown. The hard landing imposed loads beyond design strength resulting in failure of the wing structure. The left wing separated inboard of the left engine nacelle and the remainder of the aircraft rolled to an inverted position. A small fire in the right engine was quickly extin-guished.

223

Time of Accident	Date	Location	Airline	Aircraft	Aircraft Damage	Fire	Total Aboard	Crew F	S	M/N	Passengers F	S	M/N
											Division of Injury		

Scheduled Passenger Service (Cont'd)

Time of Accident	Date	Location	Airline	Aircraft	Aircraft Damage	Fire	Total Aboard	Crew F	S	M/N	Passengers F	S	M/N
0736 CST	3/26/57	Des Moines, Iowa	United	CV-340	Substantial	None	16	0	0	3	0	0	13

The crew had been advised that snow and ice on the runways caused fair to poor braking action. Following a normal touchdown in the center of the runway, the right gear rolled into drifted snow, and a yaw to the right occurred. Propellers were in reverse and the pilot increased power on the left engine in an unsuccessful attempt to regain directional control. The left propeller struck a high windrow of snow, fracturing the engine nose intermediate case, and the assembly separated from the aircraft.

| 0153 EST | 4/1/57 | Mobile, Ala. | Capital | Viscount 745D | Substantial | None | 46 | 0 | 0 | 3 | 0 | 0 | 43 |

The approach was made in rainy, turbulent conditions. Touchdown in a left skid was effected half-way down the runway. The aircraft tended to veer right, however, control was maintained without difficulty and flight taxied into the ramp. Inspection disclosed Nos. 1 and 2 propellers in the feathered position and damaged from contact with the runway.

Time	Date	Location	Operator	Aircraft	Damage					
1611 MST	4/7/57	El Paso, Texas	American	DC-6	Substantial	None	52	0 0 5	0 0 47
2010 CST	4/8/57	Birmingham, Alabama	Delta	DC-7 Parked Viscount	Minor Substantial	None	28	0 0 5	0 0 23
2101-2200 EST	4/8/57	Nr. Norfolk, Virginia	Capital	Viscount 745D	Substantial	None	20	0 0 4	0 0 16

The approach was made in a strong gusty wind with blowing dust and sand. A sudden windshift, with reduced visibility, occurred as the aircraft was flared for landing. Power was applied for a go-around. This however, was aborted when a lowered wing failed to respond to controls and the aircraft touched down, right gear first. The nose gear retracted and the aircraft rolled to a stop with the nose in contact with the runway.

As the DC-7 was being taxied out to takeoff position, its left wing tip collided with parked Viscount.

Shortly after departing Norfolk, the flight was advised of a line of precipitation across its path. Speed had been reduced when a 4-5 minute period of turbulence, hail and rain was encountered, and altitude varied from 8,000-10,300 feet. Once clear of the area, the flight continued to Washington without further incident. Subsequent inspection revealed damage to the stabilizers and elevator.

Time of Accident	Date	Location	Airline	Aircraft	Aircraft Damage	Fire	Total Aboard	Division of Injury					
								Crew			Passengers		
								F	S	M/N	F	S	M/N

Scheduled Passenger Service (Cont'd)

Time of Accident	Date	Location	Airline	Aircraft	Aircraft Damage	Fire	Total Aboard	Crew F	Crew S	Crew M/N	Pass. F	Pass. S	Pass. M/N
1525 EST	4/18/57	Pittsburgh, Pa.	Capital	DC-4	Substantial	After Impact	55	0	0	4	0	0	51

The copilot discontinued a simulated ILS approach at the middle marker and established visual reference with the runway. The captain observed the rate of descent to be excessive and immediately applied power to regain the lost altitude. Before recovery was complete the right main gear struck the embankment short of and below the edge of the runway. Full power was applied and a go-around made. Severe buffeting was experienced as the flight circled for another approach and fire occurred in No. 3 engine area. The flight landed safely and ground firefighting equipment extinguished the fire.

Time of Accident	Date	Location	Airline	Aircraft	Aircraft Damage	Fire	Total Aboard	Crew F	Crew S	Crew M/N	Pass. F	Pass. S	Pass. M/N
2340 CST	4/19/57	Dallas, Texas	Braniff	CV-340	Substantial	None	42	0	0	3	0	0	39

As the gear was retracted following takeoff, the nose gear transit light remained on. A check by ground observers showed that the nose gear was not in normal position. The flight then returned to Dallas and made a landing, the nose gear retracting aft under the fuselage.

1344 MST 4/21/57 Nr. Phoenix, Arizona   Frontier   DC-3   Substantial   None   26 | 0 0 3 | 0 0 23

The flight departed Prescott, enroute to Phoenix, flying VFR. Deteriorating weather conditions were encountered over mountainous terrain, however, and approximately 18 minutes after departure from Prescott an IFR clearance was requested. The flight was operated in solid instrument conditions for several minutes prior to the accident which occurred at about the time the IFR clearance was received. The aircraft struck a mountain ridge at an elevation of 4,600 feet resulting in considerable damage to the outer portion of the left wing. Control of the aircraft was maintained and the flight landed at Phoenix without further incident.

2158 EST 5/1/57 Muskegon, Michigan   Capital   DC-3   Substantial   None   21 | 0 0 3 | 0 0 18

While in the final part of the roll-out, during a crosswind landing, the aircraft went off the runway in a sharp left turn, slid sideways into soft sand, and sheared its left gear.

Scheduled Passenger Service (Cont'd)

Time of Accident	Date	Location	Airline	Aircraft	Aircraft Damage	Fire	Total Aboard	Division of Injury Crew			Passengers		
								F	S	M/N	F	S	M/N
0958 EDT	5/21/57	Branchville, N.J.	Capital	Viscount 745D	Substantial	None	37	0	0	3	0	0	34
1713 MST	6/1/57	Salt Lake City, Utah	Frontier	DC-3 Cessna 182A	Minor Substantial	None	9 1	0 0	0 0	2 1	0	0	7
0325 EST	6/8/57	Norfolk, Virginia	Eastern	DC-7B	Substantial	In Air	77	0	0	5	0	0	72

The lower forward cargo door separated from the aircraft in flight resulting in explosive decompression. No. 3 propeller was damaged when struck by baggage which had fallen from the compartment and severe vibration resulted. The propeller was feathered and flight returned to LaGuardia, landing without further incident.

The DC-3 had been cleared to follow the Cessna for taxi to take-off area. As the latter was stopped at the run-up, it was struck by the DC-3.

At 19,000 feet, No. 1 propeller oversped and engine fire occurred. All attempts to feather the propeller were unsuccessful and the captain ordered the engine frozen. CO_2 was discharged, but the fire continued to burn. It was extinguished by ground fire-fighting equipment following an unscheduled landing at Norfolk.

2350 CST 6/23/57 Grand Forks, N.D. North Central DC-3 Substantial None | 10 | 0 0 3 | 0 0 7

The aircraft was on final approach with landing lights on. While crossing a highway about 100 feet from the head of the runway, the right gear struck a passing tractor-trailer truck. The flight returned to Minneapolis where a wheels-up landing was made.

0133 EST 7/3/57 Atlanta, Ga. Capital Viscount 745D Substantial None | 43 | 0 0 3 | 0 0 40

The aircraft veered off the runway, striking runway lights, and damaging the propellers while landing.

0930 EDT 7/13/57 Williamsport, Pa. United DC-6B None None | 24 | 0 1 4 | 0 0 19

Airborne radar was utilized by the crew to circumvent thunder-storms enroute. Upon entering smooth air, and with the radar screen clear of any indication of storm activity, the seat belt sign was turned off. Shortly thereafter, unexpected sharp gusts were encountered, a stewardess was thrown into the aisle sustaining a fractured ankle.

229]

Time of Accident	Date	Location	Airline	Aircraft	Aircraft Damage	Fire	Total Aboard	Crew F	S	M/N	Passengers F	S	M/N

Scheduled Passenger Service (Cont'd)

Time of Accident	Date	Location	Airline	Aircraft	Aircraft Damage	Fire	Total Aboard	Crew F	S	M/N	Pass. F	S	M/N
0329 CST	7/17/57	Nr. El Paso, Texas	American	DC-6	None	None	85	0	0	5	0	1	79

Another aircraft was observed on an apparent collision course and the captain initiated an evasive maneuver. Several passengers were thrown from their seats. An unscheduled landing was made at El Paso without further incident.

| 0337 PDT | 7/25/57 | Daggett, Calif. | Western | CV-240 | Substantial | None | 16 | 0 | 0 | 3 | 1 | 0 | 12 |

While cruising at an altitude of 10,000 feet, with cabin pressurized to 4,000 feet, an explosion occurred in the lavatory followed by decompression. A large jagged hole was torn in the fuselage through which a passenger, who had exploded a charge of dynamite, was lost. The flight made a safe, unscheduled landing at George Air Force Base.

| 2059 EST | 7/28/57 | Ypsilanti, Mich. | Northwest | B-377 | Substantial | On Ground | 21 | 0 | 0 | 5 | 0 | 0 | 16 |

A fire occurred in the right wheel area as the engines were being run up preparatory to takeoff. CO2 was discharged into No. 3 na-

Time / Date	Location	Carrier	Aircraft	Damage	Injury (In Air)	Aboard	Crew Fatal	Crew Serious	Crew None	Pass. Fatal	Pass. Serious	Pass. None
1545 EDT 7/28/57	Enroute Norfolk to Washington	Capital	Viscount	None	None	47	0	1	2	0	0	44
1640 EST 8/3/57	New York, N.Y. (LaGuardia)	Trans World	L-749A	Substantial	In Air	16	0	0	6	0	0	10
0318 MST 8/6/57	Salt Lake City, Utah	Western	DC-6B	Minor	None	41	0	0	4	0	0	37

celle and as the airport emergency equipment arrived the fire was extinguished. Hydraulic fluid leaking in the brake assembly had ignited from the engine exhaust on an overheated brake.

Unexpected severe turbulence was encountered, throwing the stewardess to the floor, fracturing her forearm.

Immediately after takeoff, fire warning for No. 2 engine occurred. The propeller was feathered and CO_2 discharged and fire warning ceased. Flight returned to the airport and landed without further incident. Fire was confined to No. 2 engine assembly and nacelle.

As the Station Agent was removing the electrical energizer from its position under the aircraft, he inadvertently put it into reverse and moved into the arc of No. 2 propeller and was struck.

231]

Scheduled Passenger Service (Cont'd)

Time of Accident	Date	Location	Airline	Aircraft	Aircraft Damage	Fire	Total Aboard	Division of Injury					
								Crew			Passengers		
								F	S	M/N	F	S	M/N
1035 EST	8/30/57	Boston, Mass.	Northeast	C-46	Substantial	In Air	36	0	0	3	0	0	33

The flight was holding at intersection, awaiting descent clearance, when fire occurred in the left engine. A rapid descent was made, a single engine landing was effected without incident and the fire was extinguished by ground fire equipment.

| 1113 CST | 8/31/57 | Nashville, Tenn. | American | DC-6 | None | None | 34 | 0 | 0 | 5 | 0 | 1 | 28 |

A passenger left her seat after the seat belt sign had been turned on. She fell in the aisle when turbulent conditions were encountered, injuring her ankle.

| 1730 MST | 9/13/57 | Denver, Colo. | Western | DC-3 | Substantial | None | 20 | 0 | 0 | 3 | 0 | 0 | 17 |

While taxiing in to the gate, the right wing struck a truck being driven across the ramp. Visibility was restricted in rain, fog and near darkness.

1750 EST	9/13/57	New York, N.Y.	Trans World	L-049	Substantial	None	85	0	0	5	0	0	80

The macadam runway was wet and slippery and braking action was ineffective. The pilot attempted to turn into the paved warm-up area, but the aircraft slid off the runway, the left wing striking a windsock supporting pole.

2046 EST	9/15/57	New Bedford, Mass.	Northeast	DC-3	Destroyed	After Impact	24	2	1	0	10	11	0

The flight was cleared for an ILS approach due to low ceiling and reduced visibility in fog. The crew failed to adhere to the prescribed ILS approach procedure and the aircraft struck trees to the right of and below the glide path.

1211 EST	10/2/57	Charlottes-ville, Va.	Piedmont	DC-3	Substantial	None	17	0	0	3	0	0	14

Flight was taxiing in to the ramp when both main gears suddenly retracted. Later examination and tests failed to disclose any malfunction in the landing gear, its safety latch mechanisms or the warning systems.

Scheduled Passenger Service (Cont'd)

Time of Accident	Date	Location	Airline	Aircraft	Aircraft Damage	Fire	Total Aboard	Crew F	S	M/N	Passengers F	S	M/N
1739 EST	10/3/57	Syracuse, N.Y.	Mohawk	CV-240	Substantial	None	38	0	0	3	0	0	35

Loss of nose wheel steering was experienced as aircraft was being taxied out for takeoff. It swerved from the taxiway into a ditch before the emergency air-brake could be applied. Loss of hydraulic pressure was due to failure of the nose wheel steering unit.

Time of Accident	Date	Location	Airline	Aircraft	Aircraft Damage	Fire	Total Aboard	Crew F	S	M/N	Passengers F	S	M/N
1941 CST	10/7/57	Manhattan, Kansas	Continental	DC-3	Substantial	None	11	0	0	3	0	0	8

A considerable amount of water on the runway made braking action ineffective during landing. A groundloop was attempted but the aircraft veered into soft ground and ran into a deep drainage ditch to the right of the runway.

Time of Accident	Date	Location	Airline	Aircraft	Aircraft Damage	Fire	Total Aboard	Crew F	S	M/N	Passengers F	S	M/N
1955 PST	10/8/57	Reno, Nevada	Western	DC-6B	None	None	13	0	0	5	0	1	7

A passenger failed to heed the seat belt sign, or the announcement by captain and cabin attendant to fasten his seat belt. As a result he was thrown to the floor, when unexpected turbulence was encountered, and received a broken bone.

2108 EST 10/17/57 Pittsburgh, Northwest DC-6B Substantial None 34 | 0 0 4 | 0 0 30
Pa.

An ILS approach was being made. Shortly after passing the middle marker, the centerline approach lights and then the runway lights became visible, and the approach was continued visually. The aircraft touched down short of the runway with the gear striking the ground below the level of the overrun area. The gear was sheared and the aircraft slid down the runway on its fuselage.

0952 PST 10/31/57 Los Angeles, United DC-7 Substantial None 16 | 0 0 5 | 0 0 11
Calif.

The right main gear failed to extend and lock. The crew used all known emergency procedures in an unsuccessful attempt to lock the gear down. After all precautionary safety measures were taken by both ground and flight personnel, the aircraft was landed with the wheels retracted.

235]

Scheduled Passenger Service (Cont'd)

Time of Accident	Date	Location	Airline	Aircraft	Aircraft Damage	Fire	Total Aboard	Division of Injury					
								Crew			Passengers		
								F	S	M/N	F	S	M/N
1520 EST	11/14/57	Massena, N.Y.	Eastern	M-404	Substantial	After Impact	5	0	0	3	0	0	2

In the traffic pattern, the copilot at the controls, an over-riding wind caused the aircraft to drift closer to the airport on the base leg, resulting in a higher and closer than normal position on final. The captain took over control and made a power-off approach, descending in a steep nose-down attitude at a high rate of descent. This could not be arrested sufficiently before touch-down and the runway was contacted with great force, the right engine separating from the aircraft. Following rebound, the runway was again contacted with great force, and the aircraft then rolled off the runway to the right, the left powerplant falling free.

Time of Accident	Date	Location	Airline	Aircraft	Aircraft Damage	Fire	Total Aboard	Division of Injury					
								Crew			Passengers		
								F	S	M/N	F	S	M/N
Between 1615 & 1638 PST	11/21/57	Los Angeles, Calif.	American	DC-7	None	None	39	0	1	4	0	0	34

Severe turbulence was encountered while letting down at reduced speed. One of the cabin attendants was thrown to the floor and received serious leg injuries.

2151 PST 11/21/57 Ontario, Calif.   Western   DC-6B   Minor   None

34   0 1 4   0 1 28

While letting down and at an altitude of between 8,000 and 9,000 feet, unexpected severe turbulence was encountered. The seat belt sign had been on for some time previous to this. The two cabin attendants and several passengers had not remained seated with belts fastened and were injured in varying degrees when thrown about.

12/19/57 St. Louis, Mo.   Trans World   L-049   Substantial

83   0 0 5   0 0 78

During the landing roll, a groundloop to the left occurred. The aircraft left the runway, right main gear collapsing. (Preliminary)

Scheduled Passenger Service U.S. Foreign/Overseas Operations

2250 CST 1/18/57 New Orleans, La.   Delta   DC-7   Substantial   None

74   0 0 6   0 0 68

A mild explosive cabin decompression occurred at an altitude of 17,500 feet. The cabin depressurized as the flight made a rapid descent and returned to New Orleans, landing without further incident. Inspection revealed fuselage cracks in the area of the forward crew entrance and cargo doors.

237

Scheduled Passenger Service U.S. Foreign/Overseas Operations (Cont'd)

Time of Accident	Date	Location	Airline	Aircraft	Aircraft Damage	Fire	Total Aboard	Crew F	S	M/N	Passengers F	S	M/N
0430 AST	3/9/57	Enroute N.Y. to San Juan, P.R.	PAWA	DC-6A	None	None	50	0	0	5	0	1	44

While at an altitude of 19,000 feet, the pilot observed an unidentified flying object that appeared to be on a collision course. He immediately initiated evasive action and a number of passengers were injured when thrown from their seats.

| 2102 EDT | 5/20/57 | New York, N.Y. (International) | PAWA | DC-7B | None | None | 56 | 0 | 0 | 6 | 0 | 0 | 50 |

The aircraft was parked and a line crew mechanic, who was inserting gear landing pins, walked into a revolving propeller.

| 2132 EDT | 8/16/57 | Newark, N.J. | EAL | DC-4 | Substantial | None | 37 | 0 | 0 | 5 | 0 | 0 | 32 |

The aircraft had been taxied to the warm-up block and as the parking brakes were applied prior to engine run-up the nose gear suddenly collapsed. The nose gear piston tube had failed circumferentially above the nose wheel fork adjacent to the radius.

Time	Date	Location	Operator		Type	Damage		Aboard						

0231 CST 11/8/57 New Orleans, La. Delta DC-7 Substantial None   66 | 0 0 5 | 0 0 61

A squall line with heavy rains and strong gusty winds was passing over the airport during the landing approach. Shortly after touch-down, strong side gusts were encountered and the aircraft veered from the runway into soft ground. The nose wheel was turned as it contacted the edge of a bisecting runway, and the nose gear was sheared. The wind was 25-35 knots.

11/8/57 Enroute San Francisco-Honolulu PAWA B-377 Destroyed   44 | 8 0 0 | 36 0 0

Crashed into Pacific Ocean under unknown circumstances. (Preliminary)

1709 EST 12/12/57 New York, N.Y. PAWA B-377 Substantial Fire on Ground   41 | 0 0 10 | 0 0 31

The flight was taxiing back to the ramp after having aborted two takeoffs due to loss of power. The brakes overheated during the prolonged taxi causing the expander tubes to rupture and allow hydraulic fluid to contact the hot brake assemblies resulting in a fire on both main gears. The aircraft headed off the taxiway as normal brakes, emergency brakes, and nosewheel steering were lost and the pilot reversed the propellers on all engines to bring the aircraft to a stop.

Time of Accident	Date	Location	Airline	Aircraft	Aircraft Damage	Fire	Total Aboard	Division of Injury					
								Crew			Passengers		
								F	S	M/N	F	S	M/N
Scheduled Passenger Service U.S. Foreign/Overseas Operations (Cont'd)													
2015 AST	12/13/57	Fairbanks, Alaska	PAWA	DC-4	Substantial	None	50	0	0	5	0	0	45

The takeoff was being made by the second officer over a flat un-lighted area. As the flaps were retracted and power adjusted during transition to enroute climb configuration, the crew was not immediately aware that the aircraft was descending. Strong corrective action was initiated by the captain but not in sufficient time to avoid striking a tree with the left wing. Upon attaining cruise altitude it was found that the aircraft operated normally and since enroute conditions were favorable the flight continued to Seattle, landing without incident.

This report on aircraft accidents in 1957 is an excerpt from a Civil Aeronautics Board Bureau of Safety pamphlet entitled "Resume of U.S. Civil Air Carrier and General Aviation Aircraft Accidents, Calendar Year 1957." Forty-five accidents are listed under the heading "Scheduled Domestic Operations—Passenger Service." In statistical records the CAB lists only 43 accidents in this category for the calendar year 1957, and it is quite possible that two of the following incidents were dropped from the official list: 2/8/57 at Louisville, Ky.; 7/17/57 at North El Paso, Texas; 7/25/57 at Daggett, Calif.; or 8/6/57 in Salt Lake City.

It should be noted that the injury to crew members in the Rikers Island accident is listed in this report as "minor/none." Probably the three stewardesses should have been listed under "serious," and possibly there are other discrepancies of the sort in connection with other accidents.

THE SAFETY RECORD OF U.S. DOMESTIC AND INTERNATIONAL PASSENGER OPERATIONS

Year	Accidents		Fatalities			Passengers Carried	Passenger-Miles Flown	Passenger Fatality Rate Per 100 Million Passenger-Miles Flown
	Total	Fatal	Passenger	Crew	Total			
1938	29	7	32	22	54	1,475,122	614,459,000	5.20
1939	33	3	19	7	26	2,031,883	833,389,000	2.28
1940	35	3	35	10	45	3,208,798	1,262,395,000	2.77
1941	30	5	37	9	46	4,377,550	1,672,253,000	2.21
1942	25	5	55	16	71	3,601,926	1,741,593,000	3.15
1943	16	3	32	12	44	3,408,860	1,925,309,000	1.66
1944	31	4	65	8	73	4,488,776	2,534,028,000	2.56
1945	38	9	93	21	114	7,181,466	3,870,470,000	2.40
1946	43	11	115	34	149	13,532,109	7,198,511,000	1.60
1947	45	8	219	30	249	14,249,920	8,176,580,000	2.67
1948	64	6	103	25	128	14,540,951	8,207,539,000	1.25
1949	37	4	93	11	104	16,640,082	9,239,822,000	1.00
1950	41	6	144	21	165	19,102,905	10,701,611,000	1.34
1951	47	9	173	33	206	24,694,012	13,684,749,000	1.26
1952	45	8	140	15	155	27,376,266	16,173,441,000	0.86
1953	37	6	88	15	103	31,425,421	18,903,180,000	0.46
1954	48	4	16	7	23	35,222,667	21,294,276,000	0.07
1955	45	8	158	23	181	41,443,772	25,152,213,000	0.62
1956	48	4	143	13	156	45,689,240	28,462,696,000	0.50
1957	50	4	67	10	77	49,120,271	32,234,179,000	0.20
1958	53	6	124	15	139	48,853,324	32,497,133,000	0.38
1959	62	9	257	37	294	55,824,400	37,725,575,000	0.68
1960*	71	12	336	42	389	58,850,000	40,000,000,000	0.84

*Preliminary estimates, including 11 fatalities on the ground.

241]

ACCIDENTS AND ACCIDENT RATES IN SCHEDULED OPERATIONS[1] OF SCHEDULED AIR CARRIERS
1949–1959

| Year | Number of Accidents | | Miles Flown | Hours Flown | Accident Rates | | | |
| | Total | Fatal | | | Per 1 Million Miles | | Per 100,000 Hours | |
					Total Accidents	Fatal Accidents	Total Accidents	Fatal Accidents
1949	66	11	463,198,100	2,520,000	0.142	0.023	2.619	0.436
1950	59	6	477,463,000	2,561,900	.123	.012	2.302	.234
1951	71	16	526,589,500	2,779,900	.134	.030	2.554	.575
1952	78	10	589,430,300	3,030,800	.132	.016	2.573	.329
1953	62	8	657,093,300	3,271,900	.094	.012	1.894	.244
1954	68	7	689,782,700	3,294,100	.098	.010	2.064	.212
1955	65[a]	12[a]	779,921,000	3,672,500	.083	.015	1.769	.326
1956	72	7	869,315,000	4,031,000	.082	.008	1.786	.173
1957	74[b]	8[b]	970,168,000	4,443,500	.075	.008	1.665	.180
1958	69	10	972,988,000	4,338,900	.071	.010	1.590	.230
1959	78	14	1,030,252,000	4,503,000	.075	.013	1.732	.310

[1] Data based on all scheduled service, including cargo service of all scheduled carriers, including Intra-Alaskan carriers. Includes propeller accidents to persons.
[a] Excludes accident at Longmont, Colorado 11/1/55 involving sabotage.
[b] Excludes accident at Daggett, California 7/25/57 involving suicide of a passenger.

Civil Aeronautics Board
April 15, 1960

ACCIDENT RECORD IN THE
OVER-ALL REVENUE AND NONREVENUE OPERATIONS
OF THE CERTIFICATED AIR CARRIERS
1949-1959

Year	Number of Accidents		Aircraft Miles Flown	Accident Rate Per 1 Million Miles Flown		Fatalities		
	Total	Fatal		Total Accidents	Fatal Accidents	Passengers	Crew	Others
1949	76	13	482,707,000	0.157	0.026	100	19	4
1950	73	9	501,778,000	.145	.017	148	25	3
1951	85	20	556,763,000	.152	.035	186	46	3
1952	95	12	618,960,000	.153	.019	176	21	19
1953	71	12	685,957,000	.103	.017	113	27	4
1954	81	8	719,550,000	.112	.011	16	12	3
1955	81[a]	15[a]	819,581,000	.098	.018	158	32	6
1956	96	9	948,183,000	.101	.009	156	18	0
1957	105[b]	13[b]	1,054,241,000	.099	.012	72	18	7
1958	85	15	1,045,439,000	.081	.014	128	27	5
1959	102	18	1,150,000,000[c]	.088	.015	270	59	9

Data includes propeller accidents to persons.

[a] Excludes accident at Longmont, Colorado, 11/1/55, involving sabotage.

[b] Excludes accident at Daggett, California, 7/25/57, involving suicide of a passenger.

[c] Estimated.

December 22, 1959

Northeast Flight 823

February 1, 1957

CREW

Alva V. R. Marsh
Basil S. Dixwell
Angelo Andon

Doris Steele
Catherine Virchow
Emily Gately

PASSENGERS

Anderson, Robert Hartley
Quebec, Canada

Anderson, Mrs. Robert Hartley
Quebec, Canada

Andrews, Mrs. Barbara
Worcester, Mass.

Ball, Abraham
Brooklyn, N. Y.

Benson, Mason
New York, N. Y.

Benson, Mrs. Mason
New York, N. Y.

Benson, Mrs. Beatrice S.
The Bronx, N. Y.

Benson, Joseph S.
The Bronx, N. Y.

Bourgoin, Arthur
Augusta, Me.

Bourgoin, Mrs. Mary
Augusta, Me.

Broadfoot, Miss Joan
Valley Stream, N. Y.

Bruso, Dr. A. J.
Fitchburg, Mass.

Carty, Mrs. Marie Ruth
New York, N. Y.

Chadwick, Miss Gloria
Lowell, Mass.

Chadwick, Mrs. Laura
Lowell, Mass.

Chadwick, Norman
Lowell, Mass.

Chase, Miss Ann
Brooklyn, N. Y.

Chopelas, Mrs. Esther
Malden, Mass.

Chopelas, Gregory
Malden, Mass.

Connors, Mrs. Nora
New York, N. Y.

Davis, Norman
Roslyn Heights, N. Y.

DeRosa, Mario
The Bronx, N. Y.

Dresner, Edwin
Great Neck, N. Y.

Dresner, Mrs. Roslyn
Great Neck, N. Y.

Domash, Mrs. Barbara
Plainview, N. Y.

Domash, Eileen
Plainview, N. Y.

Domash, William
Plainview, N. Y.

Dubrowsky, S.
Quebec, Canada

Elden, Miss A.
Kew Gardens, N. Y.

Elden, Paul
Kew Gardens, N. Y.

Elden, Mrs. Paul
Kew Gardens, N. Y.

Farber, Miss Rose
Worcester, Mass.

Fox, E. K.
Lake Placid, N. Y.

Giroux, Mrs. Wilfred
Quebec, Canada

Gonsalvez, Hannibal
North Dartmouth, Mass.

Gonsalvez, Mrs. Rita
North Dartmouth, Mass.

Kandell, Harold
Brooklyn, N. Y.

Kandell, Mrs. Ann
Brooklyn, N. Y.

Kazakis, James
Manchester, N. H.

Koenig, Harold
Pleasantville, N. Y.

Kovnat, Dr. Benjamin
Kew Gardens, N. Y.

Kronen, Kenneth
Plainview, N. Y.

Kronen, Mark
Plainview, N. Y.

Kronen, Ricky
Plainview, N. Y.

Kronen, Mrs. Selma
Plainview, N. Y.

Landy, Joy
Miami Beach, Fla.

Landy, Marshall
Miami Beach, Fla.

Lassell, Gerald S.
Saugus, Mass.

Lassell, Mrs. Marilyn
Saugus, Mass.

Lassell, Roy
Saugus, Mass.

Leichman, Irving
Glen Cove, N. Y.

Leichman, Mrs. Irving
Glen Cove, N. Y.

Lessard, Joseph
Quebec, Canada

McAloon, Mrs. Helen
North Andover, Mass.

Munch, Miss Annette
Valley Stream, N. Y.

Naylor, Charles
Roslyn Heights, N. Y.

Naylor, Mrs. Charles
Roslyn Heights, N. Y.

Nixon, Mrs. Lillian
Worcester, Mass.

Nolan, John Q.
Norwich, Conn.

O'Brien, Miss Dorothy
Worcester, Mass.

O'Brien, Miss Geraldine
Worcester, Mass.

Opatowski, Dan
The Bronx, N. Y.

Opatowski, Mrs. Yetta
The Bronx, N. Y.

Peterson, David
Manchester, N. H.

Pierce, Robert P.
Mattapoisett, Mass.

Pierce, Mrs. Robert P.
Mattapoisett, Mass.

Price, Harold
Larchmont, N.Y.

Reddington, John F.
Milton, Mass.

Reddington, Mrs. John F.
Milton, Mass.

Ritman, Mrs. Rose
New York, N.Y.

Robbins, L.
New York, N.Y.

Robit, Mrs. Lillian
Kew Gardens, N.Y.

Salzer, Mrs. Doris
Worcester, Mass.

Salzer, James
Worcester, Mass.

Salzer, Karen
Worcester, Mass.

Sanger, Mrs. Joan
Scarsdale, N.Y.

Sanger, Mindy
Scarsdale, N.Y.

Schulman, Abraham
Forest Hills, N.Y.

Schulman, Mrs. Rita
Forest Hills, N.Y.

Schulman, Miss Arlene
Forest Hills, N.Y.

Schwartz, Hyman
Brooklyn, N.Y.

Smithberg, Irving
Brooklyn, N.Y.

Solomonsky, Mrs. Sandra
Syosset, N.Y.

Solomonsky, Garry
Syosset, N.Y.

Stamm, Miss Sarah
New York, N.Y.

Tabor, Harold
Mamaroneck, N.Y.

Taub, Dr. Jacob
The Bronx, N.Y.

Tannenbaum, Mrs. Pauline
Brooklyn, N.Y.

Tulowiecki, Edward
South Lancaster, Mass.

Tulowiecki, Nancy
South Lancaster, Mass.

Warren, Mrs. J.
Jamaica, N.Y.

Wein, A.
Little Neck, N.Y.

Williams, Miss Margaret
Worcester, Mass.

Wollock, Jules
Brooklyn, N.Y.

Zukowski, Mrs. Blanche
Worcester, Mass.

Acknowledgments

This book was written not by a pilot or airline official but by an air traveler who had the curiosity and the time to spend inquiring into the problems and practices of commercial aviation. The book's purpose was to give those on the outside—the passenger-public—the inside story of commercial aviation.

For an accounting in depth, the author has chosen one disaster involving many if not most of the problems faced by every airline, and one in which there were survivors to tell the story. It was chosen only because its complexity embraced so many of the common, everyday problems of aviation. Northeast Airlines was not singled out with the intent to portray it as the best or worst or the average of the nation's air carriers. Northeast Airlines of today is said to be a vastly improved organization and operation than that of 1957. Unfortunately, the management of the airline refused all requests of the author for help and co-operation in portraying it as it was in 1957 or as it is today.

The author was able, however, to learn about Northeast through various public documents and by generous interviews given by several past and present Northeast employees, who preferred to remain anonymous. To those persons who helped me in my quest for an accurate understanding of the airline and its people, I am most appreciative.

The two men who helped me continually throughout my research and writing of this book were my neighbors and friends: Stuart M. Speiser, one of the nation's outstanding aviation negligence attorneys, who made his office my research center; and David L. Toombs, senior co-pilot for United Airlines, who graciously served as my technical adviser and ground instructor on how to fly the DC-6.

The author received the help and advice of a great many experts of the Civil Aeronautics Board and the Federal Aviation Agency. Among them, I would like to express my appreciation to Oscar Bakke, George Van Epps, Joseph O. Fluet, G. Joseph Minetti, John McWhorter, Edward Slattery and Keith Wiesley.

In this connection, I would also like to thank John Groves, of the Air Transport Association of America; Jerome Lederer, director of the Flight Safety Foundation; Thomas A. Basnight, Jr., John R. McDonald and J. D. Smith, safety representatives of the Air Line Pilots

247]

Association; Rowland K. Quinn, Jr., president of the Air Line Stewards and Stewardesses Association; and Howard Maginniss, of the Douglas Aircraft Company.

In cross-checking as many facts and opinions as possible, the author conferred with several pilots, mechanics and stewardesses from airlines other than Northeast, including Eastern, National, Pan American and United. For help in meeting several airline employees on a personal basis, I am indebted to Gene Batzer, Associated Press reporter at LaGuardia Airport.

I would like to thank in particular Correction Commissioner Anna M. Kross for making certain prison records available to me for the Rikers Island section of this book. I would also like to thank John Reddy for allowing me to use the information he collected for a magazine article on the rescue phase of the accident. Police Commissioner Stephen P. Kennedy and Fire Commissioner Edward F. Cavanagh also were kind enough to give me an account of their activities on the night of the crash.

Learning the inside story of aviation was a reward in itself for the work involved, but an unexpected and unforgettable dividend was my meeting with many of the men and women who lived through this plane crash. I hope I have done justice in this book to the variety of personalities of those who relived the trauma of a plane crash for my benefit. I wish to express my deep appreciation to: Mason Benson, Mr. and Mrs. Arthur Bourgoin, Miss Gloria Chadwick, Mrs. Esther Chopelas, Norman Davis, Mr. and Mrs. Edwin Dresner, Gerald Lassell, Samuel Leider, Benjamin Kovnat, Mr. and Mrs. Kenneth Kronen, Mr. and Mrs. Charles Naylor, John Q. Nolan, Mrs. Joan Sanger, Mrs. Emily (Gately) Smith, Abraham Schulman, Dr. Jacob Taub, Edward Tulowiecki, Mrs. Mary Williams (mother of Margaret Williams) and Mrs. Blanche Zukowski.

Finally, the author would like to acknowledge his good fortune in having a brother who is one of the best editors in the country: So, thank you, Henry Moscow, for your incisive editing of this manuscript. And, thank you, Howard S. Cady, editor-in-chief of Putnam's, for leading me by the leash to the fascinating subject of aviation. And, for sustaining help and inspiration, the author thanks his co-pilot and crew at home.

ALVIN MOSCOW

STAMFORD, CONN.
JANUARY, 1961

Index

Index

Index